iea

Climate Change

**Challenging the Conventional
Wisdom**

WITHDRAWN

Edited by Julian Morris

With Contributions by:
Robert Balling
Roger Bate
Sonja Boehmer-Christiansen
Thomas Gale Moore

and with a Foreword by
Deepak Lal

Published by the IEA Environment Unit, 1997

First published in December 1997 by
The Environment Unit
The Institute of Economic Affairs
2 Lord North Street
Westminster
London SW1P 3LB

IEA Studies on the Environment No. 10
ISBN 0-255 36443-1

Many IEA publications are translated into languages other than English
or are reprinted. Permission to translate or to reprint should be sought
from the General Director at the address above.

Printed in Great Britain by
Hartington Fine Arts Ltd
Set in Times New Roman and Univers

Contents

Matter of Bureaucratic Sustainability

Foreword: Ecological Imperialism

Deepak Lal

Anyone breathing the polluted air of Delhi or Xian (and many other Indian and Chinese cities) will see the force of arguments that seek to control various forms of local pollution. However, environmentalists increasingly concentrate their efforts on restraining what they see as global pollution, rather than dealing with these local problems. The primary focus of their concerns at the moment is the industrial release of gases allegedly responsible for climate change –the so-called greenhouse gases (GHGs).[1] Most of the other aspects of their agenda, such as preserving tropical rain forests and bio-diversity, and controlling the size of the human population, follow from this.

Concentrations of GHGs have undoubtedly increased over the past 100 years and will no doubt continue to increase as emissions of them rise along with growth in global economic activity – particularly in those emerging giants India and China. In fact, on current growth trends, the Third World as a whole is expected to account for almost half the global emissions of GHGs by 2010, compared with less then one-third today. At the global summit in Kyoto, the representatives of Third World countries face their first serious confrontation with the international Green movement. There are signs that the so-called Annex 1 countries (the developed nations), led by the US, will impose emission standards on non-Annex countries – that is, the Third World.

Imposing such a brake on the burning of fossil fuels will inevitably retard economic growth. In the developing world this means slowing down the process by which agrarian economies, where land is the limiting factor of production, are converted into industrialised economies, in which energy is the limiting factor.

---

[1] These include, *inter alia*, carbon dioxide (CO_2), methane (CH_4), dinitrogen oxide (N_2O) and the chlorofluorocarbons (CFCs).

Economic historians have emphasised that it was not until the Industrial Revolution that mankind found the key to intensive growth (a sustained rise in *per capita* income). That key is fossil fuel, which provides an abundant source of energy and frees man from the limits imposed by the land. Only such intensive growth has the potential to eradicate mass structural poverty – the scourge that in the past was considered to be irremediable (*pace* the Biblical saying that the poor will always be with us). Putting the brakes on the burning of fossil fuels will consign millions of people in the developing world to continued penury.

In the past, most growth was extensive, with output growing in line with (modest) population growth. As pre-industrial economies relied on organic raw material for food, clothing, housing and fuel, the supply of which in the long run was inevitably constrained by the fixed factor, land, their growth was ultimately bounded by the productivity of land. In these organic economies, a long run stationary state, in which the mass of people languished at a subsistence standard of living, seemed inevitable.

The Industrial Revolution led to the substitution of this organic economy by a mineral-based energy economy. Coal became widely used, providing most of the heat energy of industry and, with the development of the steam engine, virtually unlimited supplies of mechanical energy. Intensive growth became possible, as the land constraint on the raw materials required for raising aggregate output was removed. The capital stock of stored energy represented by the fossil fuels allowed mankind to create a world in which mass poverty, rather than being the unavoidable lot of mankind, could be readily alleviated through intensive growth.

The alleviation of mass poverty through intensive growth is just beginning in two of the largest concentrations of poor people in the world – India and China. However, the Kyoto meeting threatens the prospects for intensive growth in these countries. Compare World Bank estimates of *per capita* energy consumption (in kilograms of oil equivalent): in 1990, China and India consumed 440 kgs, whilst in the same year the OECD countries consumed 5,179 kgs. This shows the great distance that India and China have to travel to convert their ancient organic economies into mineral-based energy economies. Any curtailment of the growth of their *per capita* energy consumption at Kyoto will condemn their millions of poor to continuing poverty.

In the long run solar energy might substitute for fossil fuels, but in the near future fossil fuels are the only option for developing countries. Thomas Schelling (1992) has estimated that to delay the doubling of CO_2 emissions by four decades will cost roughly 2 per cent of gross world product in perpetuity. This is a non-trivial cost for poor countries.

Arguments that the costs of global warming to the Third World will also be large are unconvincing. Most of these relate to effects on agriculture and the possible rise in sea levels. The best estimate of the aggregate effects of global warming on agriculture is that it will be favourable (Beckerman, 1995). As regards rising sea levels and the erosion of coastal areas; this is no worse than what is happening through normal sea erosion. The costs to the Netherlands, Bangladesh and various Pacific islands of adapting to the expected changes in sea level are trivial compared with the costs of preventing global warming. The Netherlands has been raising its dikes for centuries.

If there are serious concerns that certain poor developing countries would be unable to meet the prospective costs of adaptation, a better solution would be for the US and other donor nations to put the foreign aid money that is currently committed as a side payment, intended to persuade developing countries to reduce their carbon emissions, into a trust fund to be paid out to the victims of sea level rises – if the worst does come to pass – to help them adapt.

The derisory sum on offer as foreign aid to bribe the Third World to limit its emissions will bring little comfort to their poor. Apart from the extremely patchy record of past foreign aid in alleviating poverty, there is no prospect that the developed world would be willing to commit itself to official transfers of about four times current aid flows to developing countries in perpetuity – the sum that would be necessary if the developing countries are to be compensated for the loss of income, the primary consequence of stymied economic growth, that would result from the emissions limits.

Given the grave uncertainties surrounding the science of climate change, it would be morally reprehensible to prevent growth in the Third World by limiting emissions of GHGs. Whether and to what extent global warming will occur and what its different regional effects will be is still unknown. Even on the worst scenario no reputable scientist claims that we are faced with Apocalypse. But this does not satisfy the Greens, who argue that if there is even an infinitely small chance that doing nothing now could lead to Apocalypse, then analogous to Pascal's wager on the existence of God, we must act now to stop global warming – even though this action may in time be shown to be futile.

But is action now to curb greenhouse gases rational as an insurance policy? William Nordhaus (1993) has conducted a sophisticated cost-benefit study in an attempt to answer this question. Of the seven options considered, he finds the best to be geo-engineering (which is currently technical feasible), followed by an optimal tax policy, followed by doing nothing, and only then the various current alternatives which are part of the Green agenda–stabilising emissions, cutting them by 20 per cent and, worst of all, stabilising the climate. Moreover, the optimal tax policy, which is better than '*laissez-faire*', implies a mere 13 per cent reduction in greenhouse emissions from their *laissez-faire* level in 2075, and all this yields over '*laissez-faire*' is a 0.06 per cent increase in world annual consumption.

Given the difficulties of negotiating and enforcing global optimum taxes, not to mention the inevitable rent-seeking such *dirigisme* would entail, this is a piffling benefit and suggests that the truly optimum policy for the time being is to do nothing about global warming.[2] This will not satisfy the many groups who have been demanding emissions limits. But so be it.

A cynical interpretation of the Clinton Administration's current stand on Kyoto is that it is hoping that the Third World will not accept emission limitations and can then be blamed for the failure of the global Green mission. This creates a real danger

---

[2] [Editor's note: Furthermore, Nordhaus's model assumes damage costs to be similar to those predicted by the Intergovernmental Panel on Climate Change (IPCC), which has been criticised for over–estimating the potential impacts of climate change (see Chapters 1-3 in this volume).]

of a new era of direct or indirect Imperialism, to discharge a green variant of the 19th century's White Man's burden. The current agenda for the developing world, and for India and China in particular, is a form of eco-imperialism aimed at preventing industrialisation. In the interests of the world's poor, it must be firmly resisted.

References

Beckerman, W. (1995): *Small is Stupid*, London: Duckworth Press.

Nordhaus, W. D. (1993): 'Rolling the "DICE": An Optimal Transition Path for Controlling Greenhouse Gases', *Resources and Energy Economics*, Vol. 15(1), pp. 27-50.

Schelling, T. (1992): 'Some Economics of Global Warming', *American Economic Review*, January.

The Authors

Robert C. Balling, Jr. is Professor of Meteorology at Arizona State University.

Roger Bate is Director of the IEA Environment Unit, Director of the European Science and Environment Forum and a Member of Wolfson College, Cambridge.

Sonja Boehmer-Christiansen is Senior Lecturer in the Department of Geography and Earth Resources at the University of Hull.

Deepak Lal is James S. Coleman Professor of International Development Studies, University of California, Los Angeles.

Thomas Gale Moore is Professor of Economics at the Hoover Institution, Stanford University.

Julian Morris is Assistant Director of the IEA Environment Unit.

Acknowledgements

I would like to thank all the authors as well as several anonymous referees for their generous contributions. I would also like to thank Professor Colin Robinson and all the staff at the IEA for their help in producing this volume. Finally, I would like to thank all those who put up with me during the final stages of production.

J.M.

Introduction: Climate Change — Prevention or Adaptation?

Julian Morris

In August this year, Bruce Babbitt, US Interior Secretary, told the 3,000-or-so scientists convened for the annual meeting of the Ecological Society of America that they have a civic obligation to help convince a sceptical American public that global warming is both real and dangerous. 'We have a scientific consensus,' he said, 'but we don't have a public consensus' (Macilwain, 1997). But do we have a scientific consensus? Is global warming really happening at a dangerous rate?

Whilst politicians exhort scientists to become their public policy advocates, many scientists have been expressing reservations about the apocalyptic predictions that are made in the international political arena. In a recent survey by the Max-Planck-Institut für Meteorologie, 412 climate scientists were asked whether they thought climate change might occur 'so suddenly, that a lack of preparation could result in devastation of some areas of the world'. Only 38 scientists said that they agreed strongly, whereas 47 disagreed strongly and the majority were either non-committal or disagreed (von Storch et al., 1997).[1] Asked to comment on the statement, 'Climate change is mostly the result of anthropogenic causes', only 26 agreed strongly, whilst 42 disagreed strongly and the majority were either non-committal or disagreed (von Storch et al., 1997.). In the real world of scientific research, the debate continues about what causes climate change and what changes we should expect in the near future.

This book details a small part of that debate, focusing in particular on the problem of differentiating natural changes in climate from those induced by man. Much has been made of a statement in the 1995 report of the Intergovernmental Panel on

---

[1] See the internet site: <http://w3g.dkss.de/G/Mitarbeiter/storch/thyssen.html>

Climate Change (IPCC), which asserted that 'the balance of evidence suggests that there is a discernible human influence on global climate'. This, in and of itself, seems an innocuous enough phrase – all it says is that man has probably had some impact on the climate, which is hardly surprising considering that there are nearly 6 billion people on the planet each affecting, to a greater or lesser extent, the ecosystem in which they live. The question of interest, however, is to what extent man has influenced and is likely in the future to influence the climate. After all, the mere fact that we may have had some impact on the climate[2] is hardly sufficient to justify claims that 'man's emissions of greenhouse gases are causing dangerous global warming' – a small and transitory impact would be of little interest except as a scientific curiosity. Nor is the possibility that emissions of greenhouse gases may have caused some impact sufficient to justify drastic action to curb these emissions. The consequences of such action may be worse than the consequences of the climate change they are intended to prevent. In order to address these issues, this book also focuses on the economic and social implications of limiting emissions of greenhouse gases – in particular, the consequences of limiting emissions of carbon dioxide.

The Ever-Changing Climate

Climate change is real: from day to day, year to year, decade to decade, century to century and millennium to millennium, the climate of planet Earth has been and continues to be in flux. Moreover, according to ice core studies, the predominant direction of climate change over the past few hundred million years has been downward: global cooling, not global warming, has been the norm. Indeed, the current geological era, the Holocene – in which man ascended to civilisation – is described as interglacial (between glacials or, as they are commonly called, 'ice ages') because it has been unusually warm. For the past

---

[2] A serious debate persists on whether or not the impact of mankind on climate is discernible from comparisons of climate model outputs with actual temperature data. See, for example, Bate (1996) for a discussion of the veracity of the claim made in the IPCC Policy-makers' Summary and the possible perversion of the scientific process that it represents.

100,000 years or so the Earth's landmasses have been covered in ice more often than they have been covered in vegetation.

The Earth's climate is affected by many different factors. On a time-scale of millennia, fluctuations in global-mean temperature appear to be caused by three main factors: changes in the Earth's orbit, changes in the orientation of the Earth to the Sun and changes in the Sun's output (Kerr, 1996; Williams *et al.*, 1997). These changes may have resulted in fluctuations in global-mean temperature of up to 14°C over the past 800,000 years (Williams *et al.*, 1997). On a time-scale of centuries, the primary factor affecting the Earth's temperature appears to be the output of the sun (Hoyt and Schatten, 1993; Haigh, 1996).

On shorter time-scales, of a decade or so, many factors seem to play a role in climate change. Volcanic eruptions and natural weathering of minerals throw particles into the atmosphere, affecting cloud formation and reflecting back the sun's radiation, thereby cooling the atmosphere (Hansen and Lacis, 1990). Possibly more important are changes in the sun's output, which cause significant fluctuations in global-mean temperature (Reid, 1991; Friis-Christensen and Lassen, 1991; Posmentier *et al.*, 1997). In addition to these natural changes in climate, man's emissions of carbon dioxide and other greenhouse gases (GHGs) seem to be causing a warming of the atmosphere, whilst emissions of aerosols such as sulphur dioxide seem to be cooling the climate (Taylor and Penner, 1994; Wigley *et al.*, 1997; Posmentier *et al.*, 1997).[3] The relative importance of natural and man-made factors on climate has been the subject of intense debate. Distinguishing nurture from nature has proved to be no easy task.

The Climate Change Debate: Nature v. Nurture in the Global Greenhouse

In order to see why the debate over climate change has taken the shape that it has, it is helpful to understand a little about the

---

[3] In addition, there is a hot debate over the impact of chlorofluorocarbons (CFCs) and related chemicals; although these chemicals are relatively scarce, they have a radiative forcing effect that is many times that of any other GHG. However, CFCs are also implicated in the destruction of upper tropospheric/stratospheric ozone, which is itself a very powerful GHG. Thus the net effect is not known.

history of climate science. The first serious foray into understanding the Earth's climate began in the mid-19th century, when Jean-Baptiste-Joseph Fourier suggested that the Earth's relatively clement ambient temperature, which is on average about 15°C, is caused by the retention of infrared radiation by certain trace gases (water vapour chief amongst them). Without this 'greenhouse effect', the average temperature of the Earth would be somewhere between minus 34°C and minus 6°C, depending on one's assumptions (Houghton, 1994, pp. 21-22).

Towards the end of the 19th century, the Swedish scientist Svente Arrhenius, observed that concentrations of another greenhouse gas, carbon dioxide (CO_2), might increase as a result of industrial activity.[4] Arrhenius estimated that doubling the concentration of CO_2 in the atmosphere would lead to an increase in the global-mean temperature of between 5°C and 6°C (Arrhenius, 1896).

Little headway was made in our understanding of climate over the next half-century. In part this was because there were more pressing concerns, such as political instability, which left little room in government science budgets for esoteric work on an apparently minor issue. In part it was because a better understanding of weather and climate required more sophisticated analytical techniques than were available at that time.[5]

---

[4] Every year approximately 220 billion tonnes of CO_2 are emitted into the atmosphere globally as a result of natural and artificial processes (including decay of organic matter, breakdown of other gases, burning of forests and burning of fossil fuels). The contribution of man's emissions to this sum is approximately six billion tonnes (about 3 per cent). However, estimates suggest that only about 217 billion tonnes of this CO_2 are being re-absorbed every year, leaving an additional 3 billion tonnes in the atmosphere. At that rate, the concentration of atmospheric CO_2 will have doubled, from its pre-industrial level of about 280 parts per million (ppm), to 560 ppm by the end of the 21st century.

[5] Weather forecasting was mostly a matter of educated guesswork. Meteorologists would draw up charts of weather fronts and pressure and then project their own assumptions about the likely movements of the weather front. These guesses were barely informed by hydrogeographic information, since to use such would have required huge amounts of data and enormous investments in computation. The one attempt to make a 'scientific' prediction about the weather failed because of problems collecting and analysing sufficient data (MacRae, 1992, p. 316).

Things began to change in the late 1940s, with the invention of the first computers. In fact, the invention of the modern computer itself owes something to the demand for superior meteorological predictions. In 1946, John von Neumann was running low on funding for his computer project, so he went to the US Navy and told them that if they wanted better weather forecasts they should help fund his project. To the chagrin of John William Meachly, one of his chief rivals in the search for the ultimate calculating machine, von Neumann got his money. Meachly was not only a competitor in the race to develop the computer, he also had a rather different view about the mechanisms that were driving climate change. He thought that the weather could be predicted from sun spot cycles (the occurrence of dark spots on the sun had long been associated with warmer periods; their absence with colder spells – see p. 23) (MacRae, 1992, p. 315). Von Neumann favoured the rival hypothesis that the Earth's climate was being warmed by increases in concentrations of greenhouse gases (MacRae, 1992, pp. 17, 368).

Since it was von Neumann who got the Navy's money and von Neumann's team at Princeton who, in the early 1950s, were amongst the first to develop computerised meteorological forecasts, it is perhaps not surprising that von Neumann's favoured explanation for climate change – the build up of greenhouse gases – became the conventional focus of climate modelling.

Nevertheless, the 1950s was an era of technological optimism and von Neumann built his models not only to describe climate change but also to help affect it. He suggested that moderate global warming – of one or two degrees Celsius – should be encouraged by coating the polar ice sheets with 'microscopic layers of coloured matter' (MacRae, 1992, p.17). Vladimir Zwyorkin, one of the inventors of the modern television, weighed in with the suggestion that it might be possible to redirect hurricanes to areas where they would cause less damage by exploding atomic bombs in their path (MacRae, 1992, p. 315). Roger Revelle, pioneer of climate modelling and mentor of US Vice-President Gore, offered the less drastic suggestion that hurricanes might be burst by whitening the surface of the oceans

17

with aluminium oxide[6] (Calder, 1997, p. 38). Perhaps fortunately, none of these technocratic 'solutions' to climatic events ever went far beyond the fertile imaginations of their inventors.

Global Cooling or Global Warming?

By the mid-1970s, technological optimism had given way to environmental doom-saying: Barry Commoner (1971) and others warned that in its use of nuclear energy and fossil fuels, industrial society was laying the foundations of its own downfall (see also De Bell, 1970). With the attention of the populace thus primed to the perils of emissions of sulphur dioxide[7] and with an apparent 30-year decline in the global-mean temperature,[8] 'global cooling' was the hot topic on many climatologists' lips. The cause of this cooling – nature or nurture – was unclear, but some climatologists argued that the main culprits were sulphate aerosols, by-products of the burning of fossil fuels, which were increasing the reflectivity of clouds and thereby reducing the amount of sunlight hitting the Earth. Apocalyptic headlines[9] were generated by a few highly vocal climatologists, who claimed that such a fall in temperature might precipitate a decline into another ice age (for example, Schneider, 1976; Ponte, 1976; Bryson and Murray, 1979).[10]

By the early 1980s, it had become apparent that temperatures were not going to follow those dire predictions (indeed, the land-

---

[6] This would reduce the intake of sunlight by the ocean surface, thereby reducing the probability that its temperature would rise to the hurricane-inducing minimum of 26°C (although this figure was not calculated until 1986 – with the aid of very powerful computer simulation techniques: see Emmanuel, 1986).

[7] SO_2 had been implicated as a cause of smog and acid rain.

[8] The land-based global temperature record shows a marked cooling from about 1940 until the early 1970s.

[9] I remember thinking how strange it was, in the blistering summer of 1976, that in the not too distant future – if news reports were to be believed – requisite beach wear would be an eiderdown coat and snow goggles.

[10] The idea that increases in CO_2 might warm the Earth was not entirely dismissed by these theorists but it tended to be downplayed. For example, Schneider and Rasool (1971) argue that 'even an increase by a factor of 8 in the amount of CO_2, which is highly unlikely in the next several thousand years, will produce an increase in the surface temperature of less than 2 deg. K' (p. 138).

based data show global-mean temperature rising steadily from the late-1970s). As a result, some climatologists[11] suggested that the period of global cooling was just a temporary blip and that the longer-term trend was uncertain.[12] What were needed, of course, were better models of the world's climate. But better models require more research and bigger computers, both of which cost money. How did the climatologists go about getting this money? Following Arrhenius's example, they chose to estimate the impact of doubling carbon dioxide concentrations without including the effects of aerosols. The inevitable results were models predicting that the Earth would warm, rather than cool. To make the warming look more convincing, they began their analysis at the end of the 19th century, a particularly cold period, and used upwardly biased temperature data (Balling, 1992). The resultant predictions suggested that temperatures might rise by as much as $4.5°C$ over the next century (Houghton et al., 1990).

To the good fortune of the climatologists concerned, the Earth has appeared (in some data sets at least) to have been warming up ever since. So much so, in fact, that at the height of the sweltering summer of 1988 James Hansen, a senior scientist at NASA, announced to Congress that scientists were '99 per cent certain' that man was warming the planet and that action must be taken lest we cause irreversible damage to the world's ecosystems (Balling, 1992, p. 11).

---

[11] Climatology can be divided into roughly two branches: paleo-climatology and physical climatology. Paleo-climatologists look for patterns in the historic climate record and relate these to possible causes (such as changes in solar radiation), whereas physical climatologists look for processes that affect the current climate (such as emissions of GHGs). This division of labour, whilst perhaps beneficial in terms of the differences in skills required to carry out the work, has resulted in some confusion over what causes climate change. Most of the 'global cooling' proponents were paleo-climatologists; most of the global warming proponents are physical climatologists.

[12] Even during the late-1970s some climatologists had voiced scepticism about the prospects of global cooling – arguing that global warming was far more likely (Balling, 1992, p. 7). Bizarrely, one eminent climatologist, Stephen Schneider, seems to have managed to have fallen into both camps – writing a popular polemic on the perils of global cooling (Schneider, 1976) whilst almost simultaneously denouncing the idea in the academic literature (Schneider, 1975)!

The main reason for the concern being expressed by Hansen and a few other climatologists, such as Stephen Schneider (now Vice-President Gore's advisor), was that they believed that the global climate could and should be controlled by man. In contrast to the technophilic attitude of von Neumann and Revelle, the new breed of would-be climate engineers was distinctly technophobic. Their central thesis was that climate stability could be achieved by reducing GHG emissions, which would mean using less fossil fuel; meaning, in effect, reducing industrial output and travelling less. Whilst such a proposal may sound less silly than painting the arctic black or exploding atomic bombs in front of incipient hurricanes, the consequences are no less dramatic – indeed they may be even more so. Merely reducing the GHG emissions of developed countries to 1990 levels by 2010 (an act that would result in only a tiny net reduction in atmospheric GHG concentrations) might cost as much as 1 per cent of world output annually (see e.g. Fisher, 1997).[13] Because of the likely cost of such action, Hansen and other concerned climatologists realised that the case for climate control would have to be very strong indeed; so strong, in fact, that it should appear as though all of the world's scientists agreed that action was necessary.

Consensus? A Case of Political Science

However, Hansen's claim of scientific consensus was false – even amongst meteorologists and climatologists there was little belief that man was causing global warming. A 1991 poll of the American Meteorological Society revealed that fewer than half the members thought global warming was being caused by human emissions of GHGs and amongst those actively involved in research into climatology and publishing regularly in the peer reviewed literature, none thought man-made global warming had

---

[13] Such forecasts are of course subject to the same criticisms that are levelled at the forecasts of climate change: they are mechanistic projections based upon many simplifying assumptions about the workings of the global economy. In reality, the impact will be contingent upon the decisions of the billions of people acting in the global market-place. Nevertheless, it seems self-evident that any binding limits placed on emissions of GHGs (that is to say, limits which actually serve to alter behaviour) will tend adversely to affect the global economy.

occurred (Lindzen, 1992). Schneider was candid about the distortion of truth that he and his colleagues were perpetrating:

'[S]cientists should consider stretching the truth to get some broad-based support, to capture the public's imagination. That, of course, entails getting loads of media coverage. So we have to offer up some scary scenarios, make simplified, dramatic statements, and make little mention about any doubts we might have ... Each of us has to decide what the right balance is between being effective and being honest.' (Schneider, 1989)

The 'need' for a scientific consensus – in order to justify the enactment of the desired policies – led to the manufacture of a false consensus. In 1988, officials at the United Nations Environment Programme and the World Meteorological Organisation set up the Intergovernmental Panel on Climate Change (IPCC), with the aim of delivering this 'consensus'.

To those in the senior hierarchy of the IPCC, it was clear that action was needed; the IPCC's job was to establish what kind – how much and when.[14] The IPCC duly reported in 1990, through the 'consensual' Policymakers' Summary, that the increase in global-mean temperature over the coming century was likely to be of the order of 2°C but might be as much as 4·5°C (Houghton et al., 1990). The Summary also noted that such warming was likely to have severe adverse consequences for mankind and recommended that GHG emissions should be cut by at least 50 per cent (Houghton et al., 1990).

It was not until the publication of this first report by the IPCC that anyone thought to check whether the climate models being used to predict future changes told us anything terribly useful about the climate. When Patrick Michaels, one of the IPCC reviewers, analysed the models' performance, he found that they were not very good at simulating the past and cautioned against

---

[14] There was never any real prospect that the IPCC would be a scientific inquiry into the causes of climate change because the bureaucratic incentives were set wholly in favour of finding a causal relationship between mankind's emissions of GHGs and climate change, in order to justify the most drastic action possible. There was no real attempt to search for alternative explanations; confirmation not refutation was the guiding principle.

using them to predict the future (Michaels, 1992). In particular, the models required significant 'fudge factors' to make the simulated end points agree with the empirical data (without these fudge factors, the models simulated twice the observed global-mean temperature change), whilst the simulated short-term temperature fluctuations were completely out of synch with the observations. Tests showed that it was impossible to discern any hypothesised link between man's emissions and historic changes in climate. Technically, only about 45 per cent of changes in temperature over the past century were explained by the changes predicted by the best climate models – a straight line explains 67 per cent! (See below, Chapter 1, p. 39)

Given the poor predictive validity of the models, it may seem surprising that the Policymakers' Summary should contain such bold prognostications. In fact, it was perfectly reasonable, if by a rather twisted logic. *First*, the scientists who were put in charge of the IPCC were themselves 'believers' in global warming, so they would most likely have favoured the inclusion of models that tended to confirm their prejudices. *Second*, work on climate modelling had suddenly become politically important and was therefore receiving more government funding. Between 1990 and 1995, annual spending on climate change research by the US government alone increased from $600 million to an astounding $1·8 billion (Bray and von Storch, 1996). Had the Policymakers' Summary said something bland such as 'we don't know – don't do anything just yet', it is likely that political support for massive climate modelling projects would have declined (see below, Chapter 3).[15]

---

[15] Many scientists prefer politically funded projects because they provide them with more freedom to do their own research. This is especially true in applied fields such as climatology, where the alternative to government funding is to provide practical information to commercial interests — who want to know what the weather is going to do in the near future so that they can plan ahead. For example, coal and gas companies want to know how cold the coming winter is going to be so that they can decide how much fuel to supply. Similarly, manufacturers of sun tan lotion want to know how sunny the summer is going to be so that they can decide how much of their product they should produce. As a result, those climatologists who do not work exclusively for government tend to do consultancy work for big business. Nevertheless, this work often provides novel insights and can be an excellent way of pushing forward the boundaries of knowledge. For example, Piers Corbyn, who runs a private weather

The failure of these models to elucidate man's impact on the climate led to the search for alternative explanations for the warming that had occurred over the past century. Two Danish solar-terrestrial physicists, Eigil Friis-Christensen and Knud Lassen, knew that anecdotal evidence pointed to a link between the activity of the sun, as measured by the number of spots on its surface, and temperature on the Earth. For example, the marked decline in the Earth's temperature at the end of the 17th century, known as the Maunder minimum, coincided with a period during which there were very few spots on the sun's surface (Eddy, 1976). So, working in their spare time, Friis-Christensen and Lassen searched for a relationship between sunspots and temperature. After much trial and error, they found that, over the period 1861-1990, about 90 per cent of the changes in temperature could be explained by the changes in the length of the sunspot cycle. In other words, changes in solar activity explain the recent changes in the Earth's temperature far better than do changes in the composition of the atmosphere. The results were duly published in the world-renowned journal, *Science*, in 1991 (Friis-Christensen and Lassen, 1991). In addition, Reid (1991) found that variations in solar irradiance could explain most of the observed long-term trends in sea surface temperature since 1850.

Tom Wigley, then head of the Climate Research Unit (CRU) at the University of East Anglia, and an IPCC lead author, was sufficiently intrigued by this result to consider the implications for the CRU model. He and Mick Kelly, also of the CRU, tried mixing the two alternative explanatory factors, the sun and the greenhouse effect, in varying quantities, to establish which is more important. The best fit was obtained when the conventional greenhouse effect was excluded, leaving sunspot cycle length as the only explanatory factor (Kelly and Wigley, 1992). This test suggested that nature (in the form of the sun) was by far the dominant influence on the Earth's climate; indeed, nurture (man's actions) seemed to be largely benign.

---

forecasting service in the UK called Weather Action, was one of the first people to realise the relationship between solar activity and climate.

Nevertheless, both Wigley and the Danes knew that variations in solar output over the past century were too small to have caused the warming through radiative warming alone. In response, Wigley decided that since the greenhouse effect must be dominant, the correlation between solar cycle length and temperature must be spurious. As he put it to me, 'if one accepts the way that the climate system is believed to work, then it is inane to consider solar forcing alone' (personal communication, 1 October 1997). Thus Kelly and Wigley (1992, p. 329) concluded that 'the solar contribution to recent global-mean temperature change is much less than that due to increasing greenhouse gas concentrations and other anthropogenic effects'.

In stark contrast, Friis-Christensen and Lassen decided that the correlation between solar cycle length and global-mean temperature change was too interesting to dismiss, so they went searching for an alternative explanation as to why sunspots might be influencing the Earth's climate. Aided by a fellow Dane, Heinrik Svensmark, they found evidence that, in addition to the direct impact of changes in solar irradiance, the sun may be affecting temperatures on Earth by interfering with the incidence of cosmic rays (Svensmark and Friis-Christensen, 1997). The explanation goes roughly as follows. The Earth is constantly bombarded with particles from outer space, quaintly called cosmic rays. When these particles hit our atmosphere, they sometimes collide with water molecules, causing them to be electrically charged. The electrically charged water molecules then attract other nearby water molecules, forming a cloud. Since clouds reflect sunlight, an increase in cosmic rays means that less sunlight gets through to the ground, so the lower atmosphere (the troposphere) stays cooler. What does this have to do with the sun? Well, the sun constantly emits magnetic radiation, which deflects cosmic rays, preventing them from entering the Earth's atmosphere. Moreover, the amount of magnetic radiation being emitted by the sun seems to vary in a similar way to the variation in length of solar cycle. The result: more sunspots means more magnetic radiation, which means fewer cosmic particles entering the Earth's atmosphere, which means less cloud, which means hotter weather.

How do IPCC scientists respond to these claims? Many seem genuinely interested – concerned to push science towards new boundaries of knowledge. However, those with most to lose are utterly dismissive. Consider the reaction of James Hansen, senior scientist at NASA and the man perhaps most responsible for initiating the US public into the rites of man-made global warming. When I contacted Hansen, asking him what he thought about the solar-magnetic theory, he replied 'Theory? That's not theory, it's Rube Goldberg' (personal communication, 28 September 1997). As to the high correlation found by the Danes apparently supporting the theory, he said: 'Correlations are really not worth much. Science is based on testable hypotheses, not random correlations.' But Hansen did make one very pertinent observation: 'Beware of anyone who says one factor can explain everything.' A more cogent criticism came from Tom Wigley, who pointed out that the original data on solar cycle length used by Friis-Christensen and Lassen had been filtered, thereby reducing the significance of their regression.[16]

Given these criticisms, how can we tell nurture from nature in the global climate? Perhaps the most convincing test to date is that recently carried out by Eric Posmentier, Willie Soon and Sally Baliunas, who compared the relative importance of the Sun's impact on climate with that of greenhouse gas emissions in both a simulation and a multivariate regression (Posmentier *et al.*, 1997). In both analyses they found that the best model was one that included both solar effects and greenhouse gas emissions. The simulation model was found to explain 92 per cent of observed changes in temperature (adjusted $R^2 = 0.92$),[17] with solar forcing responsible for 0.41°C of the simulated change and GHGs for 0.31°C. The multivariate regression gave similar results, explaining 89 per cent of the variance, with solar effects accounting for 0.44°C and GHGs for 0.33°C. Both models

---

[16] However, Wigley commits a similar error himself: in a recent analysis of the causes of climate change he reports only R^2 statistics, not adjusted R^2 or F-statistics, which are necessary from the point of view of assessing model validity (Wigley *et al.*, 1997).

[17] The R^2 statistics were adjusted to take account of the reduction in explanatory power (technically, a reduction in the degrees of freedom) that results from inclusion of filters and the addition of variables.

significantly outperformed the models used by Wigley *et al.* (1997) and both had highly significant F-statistics.[18] Nevertheless, this superior model still predicted significant warming over the coming century if CO_2 levels do continue rising: a doubling of CO_2 was predicted to result in an increase in global-mean temperature of between 1.26°C and 1.33°C. These are in line with the lower estimate of the IPCC and, given the very strong explanatory power of the models, should perhaps be taken as mankind's current best estimate of the effect of doubling the concentration of greenhouse gases.[19]

Global Cooling Again?

Whilst the land-based data show an increase in the global-mean temperature over the past 20 years, data from satellites and radiosondes contradict this. In fact, the unadulterated satellite data show a small global cooling for the period 1979-1997 (see below, Chapter 1). As a result, some scientists have begun to look again at the possibility of sulphate-induced global cooling (Friend, 1997). Nevertheless, the primary focus of many physical climatologists remains the imminent threat of global warming, boosted by the rich rewards of government grants to estimate the devastating impact that this will have on mankind and the ecosystem in which we live (see below, Chapters 2 and 3).

The Impacts of Climate Change

Over the next century, the world's climate is going to change. Whether these changes will be induced by man or by some natural event we cannot say for certain. The changes may not be large; in all probability they will be small – a matter of 1°C or 2°C at most. But at no time in history has the climate stayed

---

[18] A model F-statistic provides a measure of the overall validity of a model.

[19] One significant caveat should be entered here. Almost all the models of global climate change focus on the impact of a doubling of CO_2 concentrations. However, it is by no means clear that CO_2 concentrations will ever double. Over the past hundred years, the amount of carbon dioxide emitted per unit of energy produced has fallen precipitously. There is no reason to expect that this trend will not continue (any more than there is reason not to expect that our use of energy will continue to rise, if allowed). So, it may well be the case that by the mid-part of the next century we may be producing so little CO_2 per unit of energy produced that the atmospheric concentration of CO_2 ceases to rise.

perfectly constant and it seems as certain as the (apparent) rising of the sun that the climate will change. The changes may be positive (a warming) or negative (a cooling) – we do not know. However, it is worth considering briefly what the effects might be on mankind.

Sea-Level Rise

One of the most frequently touted impacts of climate change is the thermal expansion of the oceans. This, it has been posited, would flood Bangladesh and other low-lying countries, including many islands. In fact, there is considerable debate over the expected extent of sea-level rise under the median IPCC warming. The hypothesised catastrophic impact is associated with a rise in sea-level of the order of 0.65m by 2100. This would entail a yearly rise of 5·9mm. The current rate of mean sea-level rise is approximately 1·8mm/yr (±0·3mm) (Douglas, 1991). So for the sea to rise as per the IPCC estimate would entail a tripling of this rate. Since there is no evidence that sea-level rise has been accelerating over the past 100-150 years (Baltuck, 1996), it seems a little unreasonable to suggest that the future should look so wet.

Hurricanes

Much has been made of claims in the various IPPC reports that the incidence and severity of hurricanes might increase in a warmer world. However, Balling (1997) suggests that hurricane incidence is inversely related to temperature change, so we might equally expect the opposite.

Desertification

Deserts are caused by long-term changes in vegetation patterns, driven by reductions in the precipitation/evapotranspiration (P/ET) rate. The overall impact on the P/ET rate in dry areas is unclear but historical evidence suggests that warmer periods tend to be associated with smaller deserts, suggesting that the increase in precipitation consequent on a warming of the atmosphere would outweigh the increase in evapotranspiration in the Sahel, Rajasthan, the Kalahari, the Gobi and other very dry areas (see especially Chapter 4 in this volume and Morris, 1995).

Species Loss

Some environmentalists have asserted that global warming would result in a catastrophic loss of biodiversity because species would not be able to adapt to the changing climate. If the world does warm significantly, species that have adapted to cooler weather would be forced to migrate to more latitudinous climes. However, it seems unlikely that a mass extinction would or could occur. Species are constantly evolving in response to environmental change and it seems quite plausible that the number of species could actually increase in response to global warming, especially if the amount of rainfall does increase as suggested. The most reliable evidence available – based on analysis of the fossil record going back 80 million years – suggests that mammals are peculiarly resistant to temperature change and that warming tends to increase biodiversity, not reduce it (Kerr, 1997). As Richard Kerr (1997) notes: 'A host of modern mammals from primates to ungulates abruptly appeared in North America, in time with a sudden burst of warming that may have been driven by a sharp gush of greenhouse gas from the ocean's sediments.'

Disease, Pestilence and Famine

In a chapter on public health in the 1995 IPCC Second Assessment Report (SAR), it was asserted that 'climate change is likely to have wide-ranging and mostly adverse impacts on human health, with significant loss of life' (Taubes, 1997, p. 1,004). However, many eminent epidemiologists are outraged by the tone of this report, arguing that it is largely hypothetical, is based on unjustified extrapolations and ignores the human capacity for adaptation. Epidemiologist D. A. Henderson of Johns Hopkins University, who led the international smallpox eradication programme from 1966 to 1977, queries the claim made in the IPCC report that by 2050 summer heat-waves in the United States will kill 3,000 to 6,000 people every year. As he pointed out in a recent interview in *Science*:

'They [the IPCC scientists] say, "look at what happened in Chicago a year or two ago. We had all these deaths due to heat and stroke. If the temperature rises, there will be an even greater problem." Well, good heavens, people adapt. One doesn't see large numbers of cases of heat stroke in New Orleans or Phoenix, even though they are much warmer than Chicago.' (Taubes, 1997, p. 1,005)

Similar criticisms are also made about predictions of increases in diseases. Climate change *might* cause an increase in the incidence of infectious disease. On the other hand, it might not, especially if – as is highly likely – developing countries improve their levels of sanitation. Cholera has been introduced into the US several times in the past few years but, as Fred Angulo, a medical epidemiologist at the US Centres for Disease Control, points out it did not spread 'because we have a public health and sanitation infrastructure that prevents it' (quoted by Taubes, 1997, p. 1,005). It is generally true that as countries become wealthier, their inhabitants spend more on measures to protect themselves from disease – for example by improving their water supply and sewage treatment facilities.

Agriculture

One apparently unambiguous benefit that might well result from climate change – if warming occurs primarily in winter and at night and primarily at higher latitudes (which is considered likely: Balling, 1992) – is an increase in the length of the growing season in many regions. This will enable farmers in many parts of the world who currently produce only one summer crop to produce two, thereby significantly increasing yields. The increase in atmospheric carbon dioxide concentrations is also likely to increase crop yields and tree growth (Idso, 1991). As a result, the amount of atmospheric carbon dioxide absorbed each year is likely to increase, partially offsetting the increase in emissions (*ibid.*).

Assessing the Costs and Benefits of Climate Change Impacts

Whilst it is relatively easy to talk vaguely about the potential impacts of climate change under various scenarios, it is rather more difficult to make any accurate assessment of the costs of those impacts. It is harder still to weight the probability of the various scenarios occurring. And it is therefore practically impossible to come up with a weighted estimate of the cost or benefit of climate change. Moreover, even if such a figure could be obtained, it would not tell us about the distribution of the impacts of climate change.

As the above discussion and Thomas Gale Moore's elegant analysis of the history of human adaptation in Chapter 4 suggest, the balance of evidence indicates that climate change will benefit the human species. Mild winter warming would lengthen the growing season in many countries, increasing agricultural output. Increases in precipitation in arid regions would lead to a greater level of vegetative cover, raise food production levels and increase biodiversity. In short, almost everybody would be healthier and wealthier. If people in low-lying regions do have to build bigger defences or move home as a result of human-induced climate change, it is reasonable to argue that those people who benefit from the use of fossil fuel and other GHG emitting activities should contribute to their expenses. However, until such time as it becomes clear that sea-level rise is accelerating as a result of man-made global warming, it would be rash to begin such defensive activities.

Dealing with Uncertainty — Prevention or Adaptation?

When challenged with the questionable validity of climate change forecasts, environmentalists tend to adopt one of two stances. First, they assert that Bill Clinton, Helmut Kohl, or Tony Blair accepts that climate change is real. This is easily countered by pointing out that none of these people is expert in meteorology or climatology and probably is only going on the limited advice provided by their scientific advisors. They, in turn, are merely regurgitating a particular interpretation of the Policymakers' Summary of the IPCC report, which itself fails to mention many of the caveats that are contained in the main report, which does not include mention of the results of research by various scientists indicating that there are alternatives to the conventional greenhouse forcing theory.

At this point, the environmentalist will almost certainly bring up 'The Precautionary Principle', which loosely says 'prevent any action that might have serious consequences'. They will argue that 'dangerous' global warming might occur: sea levels might rise; the number and severity of hurricanes might increase; Africa might become desertified; millions of species might be wiped out because they cannot adapt to rapid climate change. What they will not mention is the probability of these events happening, or for that matter the probability of the opposite happening. That is the problem with the precautionary principle.

Applying the precautionary principle to global warming, we have something akin to an environmental version of Pascal's wager: the probability of warming occurring is irrelevant, since the benefits of taking action could be infinite, whilst the costs of taking action are tiny. But this reasoning is wrong-headed. All manner of things may have an infinite pay-off – for example, protecting the planet from an alien invasion, or a direct hit by a comet – yet we do not invest billions of dollars in such protection. Moreover, there are probably thousands of other events of which we are unaware that have a very low probability of occurring and yet would be devastating to life on Earth. These we simply could not prevent.[20]

What the environmentalists often forget is that there is an alternative to prevention – adaptation. Moreover, prevention has an opportunity cost. There is no such thing as a free climate stabilisation policy.[21] If it is cheaper to adapt to something, then

---

[20] Here, it is worth noting the difference between an uncertainty, such as climate change, and a risk, such as the flooding of the Thames. Uncertainties cannot be predicted – we may make some statements about the general direction of global-mean temperature and the possible consequences for particular regions of the world but these are all clouded in debate – whereas risks are quantifiable: the Thames has flooded regularly in the past (about twice per century) so the probability of it occurring in any single year, based on past experience, is one in fifty. However, we cannot say with any degree of accuracy what the future climate will be like. Climate change is uncertain. We cannot extrapolate from the past because there are factors affecting past climate, especially solar irradiance, which cannot be predicted (at the moment).

[21] Some economists have argued that there is a 'double dividend' from certain so-called 'no-regrets' policies. This double dividend supposedly arises because action to prevent emission of greenhouse gases also prevents other unpleasant actions, such as road congestion and other forms of urban pollution. Such claims are misleading, however, because they obscure the opportunity cost of taking action and ignore the alternative mechanisms for achieving the other environmental objectives. A petrol tax is a very inefficient means of reducing road traffic. People are relatively insensitive to increases in the cost of fuel and the tax increase harms most those people who travel furthest, who are generally not those travelling within towns and who generally do not have any alternative means of transport (or for whom the alternative is far less convenient). A

31

why try to prevent it? Ironically, this is exactly what environmentalists have been arguing in favour of with regard to wetlands conservation: do not attempt to prevent the encroaching salt marsh, simply move house. Experience suggests that the human species is remarkably good at adapting to different environments – especially warmer environments (see e.g. Boserup, 1988, and Chapter 4 in this volume) – so why are we trying to put the brakes on nature?

We do not know whether our emissions of carbon dioxide, methane and other 'greenhouse gases' might have serious consequences for the future. What we do know is that limiting emissions of these gases would be likely to reduce the productivity of practically every economy in the world. Such limits would not only reduce average incomes but would cause many people to lose their jobs and would force millions of others to remain in abject poverty. Moreover, this enforced impoverishment would reduce our ability to adapt to a changing world, both because of the increase in the choice set that comes about with increased wealth and because of the increase in technology that comes about as a result of people making uncoerced investments. If we are really worried about climate change, we should ensure that our children and our children's children are best able to adapt to the world in which they find themselves living.

---

much more sensible means of reducing road congestion and urban pollution is to introduce a system of road pricing which actually discouraged people from using congested roads. This would be both more efficient and more equitable than increasing fuel prices.

References

Arrhenius, S. (1896): 'On the Influence of Carbonic Acid in the Air Upon the Temperature of the Ground', *Philosophical Magazine*, Vol. 41, pp. 237-276.

Balling, R. C. (1992): *The Heated Debate*, San Francisco: Pacific Research Institute.

— (1997): 'The Spin on Greenhouse Hurricanes', in Bate (1997).

Baltuck, M., Dickey, J., Dixon, T., and Harrison, C. G. A. (1996): 'New Approaches Raise Questions about Future Sea Level Rise' (cited by Landscheit, 1997).

Bate, R. (1996): 'The Political Economy of Climate Change Science – A Discernible Human Influence of Climate Documents?', Environment Briefing Paper No. 1, London: Environment Unit, Institute of Economic Affairs, July.

— (ed.) (1997): *Global Warming: The Continuing Debate*, Cambridge: European Science and Environment Forum.

Boserup, E. (1988): 'Environment, Population, and Technology in Primitive Societies', in Worster, D. (ed.), *The Ends of the Earth*, Cambridge: Cambridge University Press, pp. 23-38.

Bray, D. and von Storch, H. (1996) 'Inside Science: A Preliminary Investigation of the Case of Global Warming', Hamburg: Max-Planck-Institut für Meteorologie Report No. 195, May.

Bryson, R. A. and Murray, T. J. (1979): *Climates of Hunger*, Madison, Wisconsin: University of Wisconsin Press.

Calder, N. (1997): *The Manic Sun – Weather Theories Confounded*, London: Pilkington Press.

Commoner, B. (1971): *The Closing Circle – Nature, Man and Technology*, New York: A. E. Knopf.

De Bell, G. (1970): *The Environmental Handbook*, New York: Ballantine/Friends of the Earth.

Douglas, B.C. (1991): 'Global Sea-Level Rise', *Journal of Geophysical Research*, Vol. 96, p. 6,981.

Eddy, J. A. (1976): *Science*, Vol. 192, pp. 1,189-1,202.

Emsley, J. (ed.) (1996): *The Global Warming Debate*, Cambridge: European Science and Environment Forum.

Emmanuel, K. A. (1986): 'An Air-Sea Interaction Theory for Tropical Cyclones. Part I: Steady-State Maintenance', *Journal of the Atmospheric Sciences*, Vol. 9, pp. 2,880-2,888.

Fisher, B. (1997): 'The Economic Impact of International Climate Change Policy', paper presented at CEI conference on the Costs of Kyoto, Competitive Enterprise Institute, Washington DC, June.

Friend, T. (1997): 'Team of Scientists Looks at New Phenomenon of Global Cooling', *The Detroit News*, 10 September.

Friis-Christensen, E. and Lassen, K. (1991): 'Length of the Solar Cycle: an indicator of solar activity closely associated with climate', *Science*, Vol. 249, pp. 698-700.

Haigh, J. D. (1996): 'The Impact of Solar Variability on Climate', *Science*, Vol. 254, pp. 981-984.

Hansen, J. E. and Lacis, A. A. (1990): 'Sun and Dust versus Greenhouse Gases: An Assessment of their Relative Roles in Global Climatic Change', *Nature*, Vol. 346, p. 713.

Houghton, J. T. (1994): *Global Warming: the Complete Briefing*, Oxford: Lion Books.

Houghton, J. T., Jenkins, G. J. and Ephraums, J. J. (1990): *Climate Change — The IPCC Scientific Assessment*, Intergovernmental Panel on Climate Change, Cambridge: Cambridge University Press.

Hoyt, D. V. and Schatten, K. H. (1993): 'A Discussion of Plausible Solar Irradiance Variations, 1700-1992', *Journal of Geophysical Research*, Vol. 98, pp. 895-906.

Idso, S. (1991): 'The Aerial fertilisation effect of CO_2 and its implications for global carbon cycling and maximum greenhouse warming', *Bulletin of the American Meteorological Society*, Vol. 72, pp. 962-965.

Kelly, P. M. and Wigley, T. M. L. (1992): 'Solar Cycle Length, Greenhouse Forcing and Global Climate', *Nature*, Vol. 360, pp. 328-30.

Kerr, R.A. (1996): 'Millenial Climate Oscillation Spied', *Science*, Vol. 271, p. 146.

— (1997): 'Climate-Evolution Link Weakens', *Science*, Vol. 276, p. 1,968.

Landscheit, T. (1997): 'Global Warming or Little Ice Age?', in Bate (1997).

Lean, J. and Rind, D. (1994): 'Solar Variability Implications for Global Change', *EOS, Transactions, American Geophysical Union*, Vol. 75 (1), pp. 4-7.

Lindzen, R. (1992): 'Global Warming: The Origin and Nature of the Alleged Scientific Consensus', OPEC seminar on the environment, Vienna, 13-15 April.

Macilwain, C. (1997): 'Ecologists Urged to "Win Climate Debate"', *Nature*, 21 August 1997 (Internet edition).

MacRae, N. (1992): *John von Neumann*, New York: Pantheon Books.

Michaels, P. J. (1992) *Sound and Fury*, Washington, DC: Cato Institute.

— and Knappenberger, P. C. (1994): 'The United Nations Intergovernmental Panel on Climate Change and the Scientific "Consensus" on Global Warming', in Emsley (1996), pp. 158-178.

Morris, J. (1995): *The Political Economy of Land Degradation*, IEA Studies on the Environment No. 5, London: Environment Unit, Institute of Economic Affairs.

Ponte, L. (1976): *The Cooling*, Englewood Cliffs, New Jersey: Prentice-Hall.

Posmentier, E., Baliunas, S. and Soon, W. (1997): 'The Relative Impact of Solar Irradiance Variations and Greenhouse Changes on Climate, 1880-1993', in Bate (1997).

Reid, G. C. (1991): 'Solar Total Irradiance Variations and the Global Sea Surface Temperature Record', *Journal of Geophysical Research*, Vol. 96, pp. 2,835-2,844.

Schneider, S. H. (1975): 'On the Carbon Dioxide-Climate Confusion', *Journal of the Atmospheric Sciences*, Vol. 32, pp. 2,030-2,036.

— (1976): *The Genesis Strategy*, New York: Plenum Press.

— (1989): Interview, *Discover Magazine*, October, p. 47.

Schneider, S. H. and Rasool, S. (1971): 'Atmospheric Carbon Dioxide and Aerosols – Effects of Large Increases on Global Climate', *Science*, Vol. 173, pp. 138-41.

von Storch, H., Bray, D. and Stehr, N. (1997): 'Perspectives of Climate Scientists on Global Climate Change', preliminary results available on the Internet site <http://w3g.gkss.de-/G/Mitarbeiter/storch/thyssen.html>.

Svensmark, H. and Friis-Christensen, E. (1997): 'Variation of Cosmic Ray Flux and Global Cloud Coverage – A Missing Link in Solar-Climate Relationship', *Journal of Atmospheric and Terrestrial Physics* (in press).

Taubes, G. (1997): 'Apocalypse Not', *Science*, Vol. 278, pp. 1,004-1,006.

Taylor, K. E. and Penner, J. E. (1994): 'Response of the Climate System to Atmospheric Aerosols and Greenhouse Gases', *Nature*, Vol. 369, pp. 734-737.

Wigley, T. M. L., Jones, P. D. and Raper, S. C. B. (1997): 'The Observed Global Warming Record: What Does it Tell Us?', *Proceedings of the National Academy of Sciences*, Vol. 94, pp. 8,314-8,320.

Williams, D.F., Peck, J., Karabanov, E.B., Prokopenko, A.A., Kravchinsky,V., King, J. and Kuzmin, M.I. (1997): 'Lake Baikal Record of Continental Climate Response to Orbital Isolation During the Past 5 Million Years', *Science,* Vol.278, pp.1,114-17.

1. Climate Model Simulations Versus Climate Reality — The Heated Debate Continues

Robert C. Balling, Jr.

In March, 1995, delegates in Berlin attending the First Conference of the Parties to the Framework Convention on Climate Change received a document showing the results from a numerical climate experiment conducted in the United Kingdom (Climate Prediction Group, 1995). One of the plots in that document showed the model output for global temperatures from 1860 to 2050 (see Figure 1.1). These results came from a numerical simulation that included both the warming effects of increasing greenhouse gases coupled with the cooling effects of sulphate aerosols. The plot also showed the actual planetary temperatures from 1860 to the near present as measured from thermometres around the world.

The scientists who prepared the report claimed that for the first time a climate model 'has been able to replicate in broad terms the slow rise in global temperature since the middle of the last century'. The obvious implication is that a model capable of simulating past conditions should be more reliable in its climate predictions for the future. By 2050, this model run shows a rise in global temperature of 1.5°C; warming in the Arctic exceeds 3°C, and a temperature increase in the United States of over 1°C. The rate of warming is 'probably twice the rate which some of the more sensitive ecosystems can tolerate'.

These same results have now appeared in major scientific journals (for example, Mitchell *et al.*, 1995), thereby furthering their impact on the greenhouse issue. Shortly after the release of these results, other scientists rather quickly followed with claims that the new and improved models simulating both sulphate increases and greenhouse gas increases could replicate observed climate patterns, not just at the surface, but throughout the atmosphere (Santer *et al.*, 1996; Hegerl *et al.*, 1996). As with virtually every element in the greenhouse debate, these claims received significant press coverage whilst in the professional journals, the claims were under attack (Michaels and Knappenberger, 1996; Weber, 1996). Many significant questions remain about the quality of all models, and the correspondence between the model output and the actual climate record is weak. Despite claims to the contrary, the models cannot simulate the observed temperature record with much accuracy; in fact, the gap may be widening.

Figure 1.1

UKMO Model Run for Increasing Greenhouse Gases and Sulphate Aerosols (thin line) from 1860 to 2050, and Actual Near-Surface Global Temperature (thick line) from 1890 to 1996

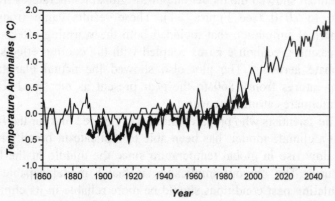

Simulated Versus Observed Global Temperatures

Two different data sets are plotted in Figure 1.1. One time-series represents the simulated planetary temperatures that result from a combination of increasing emissions of greenhouse gases and sulphur dioxide. These calculations were made by an excellent numerical climate model at the Hadley Centre in Bracknell, England; the model includes detailed representations of the atmosphere, oceans, ice, and vegetation. The calculations required to produce these two time-series took three months to run on one of the world's fastest supercomputers. The second time-series in Figure 1.1 is made up of the actual near-surface global air temperatures determined from thermometers located throughout the world (Jones, 1994). Despite substantial efforts to avoid known problems, this temperature record is still affected by urban warming, measurement errors, instrument differences, and the lack of data from many remote areas, including the oceans.

In theory, the model run with greenhouse gas and sulphate perturbations should resemble the actual temperature record, and at first glance, the correspondence is fairly good. The agreement is particularly strengthened from the late 1970s to the present when an accelerated upward trend appears in both simulated and actual temperature levels.

To be more precise, the correlation (R^2) between the simulated and observed temperatures over the entire 107-year period (1890-1996) is 0.45; the model appears to explain 45 per cent of the inter-annual variance in near-surface global temperatures. While that may seem impressive at first glance, consider that a simple line with a slope of 0.56°C per century has a R^2 of 0.67 with the observed temperature data; it explains 67 per cent of the variance in global near-surface air temperatures. A simple line explains significantly more variance in the inter-annual global temperature pattern than the numerical climate model at the Hadley Centre.

Satellite-Based Global Temperatures

The further back in time we go, the less confidence we have in the estimation of global temperature. As we move toward the most recent decades, other data sets are available to represent global temperature. One data set is derived from satellite-based measurements of microwave emissions from molecular oxygen in the lower atmosphere. The data set is accurate to within a few hundredths of a degree, and the polar orbits of the satellites assure true global coverage (see Spencer and Christy, 1990).

The comparison of simulated temperatures, global near-surface temperatures from thermometres, and the satellite-based measurements is presented in Figure 1.2. The temperatures from the model and the satellite-based lower-tropospheric temperatures are negatively related. The correlation (R^2) between the two data sets is only 0.08; the satellite-derived data actually cool while the model predicts warming. One may argue that the satellites are measuring the lower six kilometres of the atmosphere and the simulated temperatures are for the near-surface, but the models predict more warming in the lower-troposphere than they do for the surface. The actual gap between modelled and observed lower-tropospheric temperatures is greater than the gap implied in Figure 1.2.

Figure 1.2

UKMO Model Run for Increasing Greenhouse Gases and Sulphate Aerosols (thin line), Observed Near-Surface Global Air Temperature (closed boxes), and Satellite-Based Lower-Tropospheric Temperatures (open circles), 1975–2005

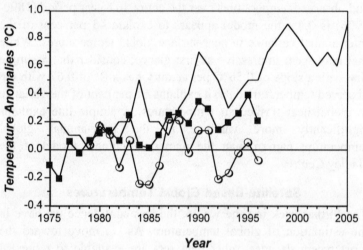

Several key papers have appeared in the literature challenging the accuracy and reliability of these satellite-based data (Hansen et al., 1995; Prabhakara et al., 1995; Hurrell and Trenberth, 1997). However, three facts show us that the satellite data are extremely accurate. First, satellite data are highly correlated with thermometer readings taken over the United States, Europe, and eastern Australia (Basist et al., 1995; Balling, 1996). The places in the world where we think we have the best near-surface air temperature data are in excellent agreement with the satellite data. There is little reason to believe that the satellite system suddenly loses its accuracy once it leaves the borders of these key test areas.

Figure 1.3

Scattergram Comparing Global Temperature Anomalies from Satellites-Based and Radiosonde-Based Measurements from 1979 to 1996

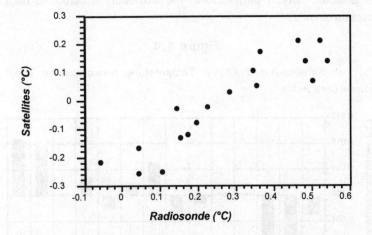

A second data set also confirms the accuracy of the satellites. Twice each day, balloons are launched simultaneously throughout the world. In a highly co-ordinated effort, radiosondes relay back their measurements of temperatures, winds, and moisture at selected heights in the atmosphere. During the period of overlapping records (1979-1996), the satellite data and the radiosonde data for the lower troposphere have a high correlation ($R^2 = 0.84$), as shown in Figure 1.3, and they show similar negative trends (-0.05°C per decade for the radiosonde data, -0.04°C per decade for the satellite data). Christy (1995) presents an excellent review of the relation of these two data sets.

Another test of the quality of the satellite data involves determining planetary temperature fluctuations throughout the lunar cycle (Balling and Cerveny, 1995). During a full moon, the moon reflects and radiates a small, but not insignificant quantity of energy to the earth. During a new moon, no energy is reflected

reflected to the Earth, and a trivial amount of energy is emitted towards the Earth. A rather easy calculation will show that the Earth should heat by a few hundredths of a degree during a full moon as compared to a new moon. Just as expected, the satellite-based temperatures warm by 0.02°C during a full moon over the temperatures experienced during a new moon (Figure 1.4). The precise determination of the lunar impact on global temperatures is possible only if the satellites are extremely accurate in their measurements.

Figure 1.4

Plot of Satellite-Based Global Temperature Anomalies by Lunar Phase Categories

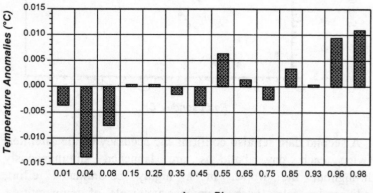

The satellite-based planetary temperature data are extremely accurate, and the satellite record does not show the warming signal that should be easily identifiable since 1979. Even when the potential effects of volcanism and El Niño/La Niña are taken into account, only a small warming of less than 0.1°C per decade can be determined from the satellite records (Christy and McNider, 1994). Furthermore, the first half of 1997 has been cold according to the satellites, despite the warming effects of an ongoing El Niño and the lack of any major volcanic eruption.

Warming in the Arctic?

Another simple test exists for evaluating the performance of the latest numerical climate model results. Virtually all numerical model runs, including the latest ones from the Hadley Centre, predict greatest warming in the northern hemispheric Arctic region, particularly in winter. In the long run, the warm-up in the Arctic is due to melting snow and the exposure of darker soil surfaces below the snow pack. In the short run, the warming is due to the greenhouse enhancement of cold and dry Arctic air that is minimally impacted by the greenhouse effect of naturally-occurring water vapour.

Figure 1.5

Arctic Annual Temperature Anomalies for 1948 to 1996 from Near-Surface Thermometer Measurements (thin line) and for 1979-1996 from the Satellite-Based Measurements (thick line)

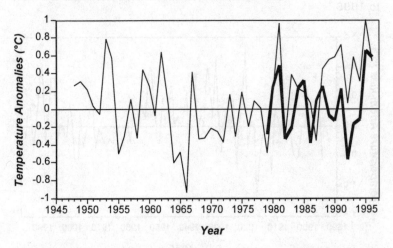

However, the Arctic as a whole is not warming much at all. Due to two recent warm years in these high latitudes, the satellite record for the Arctic shows a linear warming of 0.10°C per decade since 1979, but the warming is not statistically significant. Kahl *et al.* (1993a, 1993b) showed that over the past four decades, no trend upward could be found in radiosonde measurements in the Arctic. The near-surface air temperatures of Jones (1994) show a small, but not statistically significant, warming of 0.08°C per decade in the Arctic from 1948 to the present (Figure 1.5). There is no signal that remotely approaches the warming that should be apparent in the northern hemispheric Arctic area.

Warming in the United States?

The conterminous United States represents approximately 1.5 per cent of the Earth's surface. However, it has a mid-latitude location for which the numerical climate models show significant warming given the build-up of greenhouse gases and the increase in sulphate aerosols. The United States has a relatively good long-term temperature record from stations that largely escape the influences of urbanisation.

Figure 1.6

Conterminous United States Temperature Anomalies (°C) from 1895 to 1996

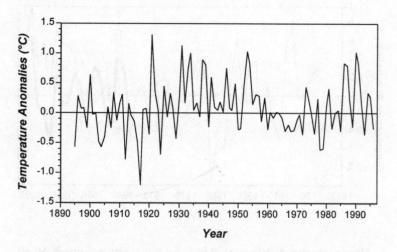

Figure 1.6 shows that over the period 1895 to 1996, the conterminous United States warmed slightly at a rate of 0.01°C per decade; the rate of warming is not statistically significant. However, the plot shows that virtually all of the warming occurred from 1915 to 1930. If we examine only the records from 1931 to 1996, we find that the conterminous United States cooled at a statistically significant rate of 0.06°C per decade!

Conclusions

The recent results from the Hadley Centre are interesting, and they certainly represent steps in the right direction in estimating the climate future of the planet. Unlike so many numerical experiments in the past, the model is now being perturbed by the combined effects of greenhouse gases and sulphate aerosols. Also, model results are being compared directly to observed climate variations during the period of historical records. However, many discrepancies still exist when the model predictions are compared to historical data.

The Hadley Centre scientists are to be commended for their quality modelling efforts. These scientists know the strengths and weaknesses of both the design of the numerical model and its ability to replicate the climate of the past century. The more one compares the model outputs to the observed climate variations, the less agreement exists between the two. The Hadley Centre experiments may be fantastic achievements in applied atmospheric physics, computer science, and applied mathematics, but little confidence should be placed in their climate prediction for the middle of the next century.

Since the publication of the fundamental results from the Hadley Centre model, several other developments have further undermined our confidence in the predictions for the future. First, the troublesome flux adjustments in the models (sometimes referred to as 'fudge factors') are now being reduced in the models, and to date, their elimination has produced a sizeable reduction in the simulated heating rates (Gregory and Mitchell, 1997). Second, Tegen et al. (1996) reported that mineral aerosols in the atmosphere (dust), coming largely from disturbed surfaces in drylands, may be producing a substantial cooling effect near the Earth's surface. Their results indicated that the mineral aerosol effect could be completely counteracting the warming effects of the build-up of greenhouse gases. Finally, some leading scientists are now arguing that sulphates may not be so important in retarding warming, but that ozone depletion may have an important negative thermal forcing at the Earth's surface (Hansen et al., 1997). The bottom line is that it is no longer fashionable simply to double carbon dioxide alone – as seen in Figure 1.7, scientists now realise that many different natural and anthropogenic activities are influencing global climate, and will continue to influence our climate long into the future.

Figure 1.7

Radiative Thermal Forcing (Wm^{-2}) for Selected Natural and Anthropogenic Influences on Global Climate over the Approximate Period 1850 to Present (from Houghton *et al.*, 1996)

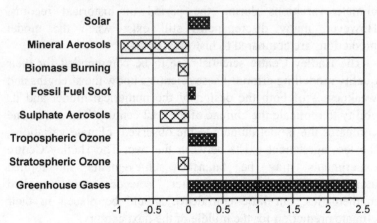

Global Radiative Forcing (Watts/Square Metre)

Nonetheless, if the models are correct, we have a problem on our hands, and substantial changes in climate can be expected to occur in the coming century. If we choose to believe in the near-surface global air temperature estimates, recent warming and record-breaking temperatures would support the low-end model predictions. Examination of the satellite-based global temperatures suggests that the atmosphere is not behaving according to the numerical climate models, and that the threat of global warming is relatively small. Regional climate patterns, particularly the general lack of warming in the Arctic or the lack of warming in the United States, also argue against the greenhouse threat. Continued combined efforts between the numerical modellers and the scientists dealing with historical records of climate will prove extremely useful in determining the fate of the climate system in the next century.

References

Balling, R. C. Jr. (1996): 'Geographic analysis of differences in trends between near-surface and satellite-based temperature measurements', *Geophysical Research Letters,* Vol. 23, pp. 2,939-2,941.

Balling, R. C. Jr. and Cerveny, R. S. (1995): 'Influence of lunar phase on daily global temperatures', *Science,* Vol. 267, pp. 1,481-1,483.

Basist, A. N., Ropelewski, C. F. and Grody, N. C. (1995): 'Comparison of tropospheric temperature derived from microwave sounding unit and the National Meteorological Center analysis', *Journal of Climate,* Vol. 8, pp.668-681.

Christy, J. R. (1995): 'Temperature above the surface layer', *Climatic Change,* Vol. 31, pp.455-474.

Christy, J. R. and McNider, R. T. (1994): 'Satellite greenhouse signal', *Nature,* Vol. 367, p.325.

Climate Prediction Group (1995): 'Modelling Climate Change, 1860-2050', Hadley Centre, Meteorological Office, Bracknell, England.

Gregory, J. M. and Mitchell, J. F. B. (1997): 'The climate response to CO_2 of the Hadley Centre coupled AOGCM with and without flux adjustment', *Geophysical Research Letters*, Vol. 24, pp. 1,943-1,946.

Hansen, J., Sato, M. and Ruedy, R. (1997): 'Radiative forcing and climate response', *Journal of Geophysical Research,* Vol. 102, pp. 6,831-6,864.

Hansen, J., Wilson, H., Sato, M., Ruedy, R., Shah, K., and Hansen, E. (1995): 'Satellite and surface temperature data at odds?', *Climatic Change,* Vol. 30, pp. 103-117.

Hegerl, G. C., Von Storch, H., Hasselmann, K., Santer, B. D., Cusbasch, U. and Jones, P. D. (1996): 'Detecting greenhouse-gas-induced climate change with an optical fingerprint method', *Journal of Climate,* Vol. 9, pp. 2,281-2,306.

Houghton, J. T., Meira Filho, L. G., Callander, B. A., Harris, N., Kattenberg, A., and Maskell, K. (eds.) (1996): *Climate Change 1995: The Science of Climate Change*. Cambridge, England: Cambridge University Press.

Hurrell, J. W. and Trenberth, K. E. (1997): 'Spurious trends in satellite MSU temperatures from merging different satellite records', *Nature*, Vol. 386, pp. 164-170.

Jones, P. D. (1994): 'Hemispheric surface air temperature variations: A reanalysis and an update to 1993', *J. Climate*, Vol. 7, pp. 1,794-1,802.

Kahl, J. D., Charlevoix, D. J., Zaitseva, N. A., Schnell, R. C. and Serreze, M. C. (1993): 'Absence of evidence for greenhouse warming over the Arctic Ocean in the past 40 years', *Nature*, Vol. 361, pp. 335-337.

Kahl, J.D.W., Serreze, M. C., Stone, R. S., Shiotani, S., Kisley, M. and Schnell, R. C. (1993): 'Tropospheric temperature trends in the Arctic: 1958-1986', *Journal of Geophysical Research*, Vol. 98, pp. 12,825-12,838.

Michaels, P. J. and Knappenberger, P. C. (1996): 'Human effect on global climate?', *Nature*, Vol. 384, pp. 522-524.

Mitchell, J. F. B., Johns, T. C., Gregory, J. M. and Tett, S. F. B. (1995): 'Climate response to increasing levels of greenhouse gases and sulphate aerosols', *Nature*, Vol. 376, pp. 501-504.

Prabhakara, C., Nucciarone, J. J. and Yoo, J.-M. (1995): Examination of 'Global atmospheric temperature monitoring with satellite microwave measurements: 1) Theoretical considerations', *Climatic Change*, Vol. 30, pp. 349-366.

Santer, B. D., Taylor, K.E., Wigley, T. M. L., Johns, T. C., Jones, P. D., Karoly, D. J., Mitchell, J. F. B., Oort, A.H., Penner, J. E., Ramaswamy, V., Schwarzkopf, M.D., Stouffer, R. J. and Tett, S. (1996): 'A search for human influences on the thermal structure of the atmosphere', *Nature*, Vol. 382, pp. 39-46.

Santer, B. D., Taylor, K.E., Wigley, T. M. L., Penner, J. E., Jones, P. E. and Cubasch, U. (1995): 'Towards the detection and attribution of an anthropogenic effect on climate', *Climate Dynamics,* Vol. 12, pp. 77-100.

Spencer, R. W. and Christy, J. R. (1990): 'Precise monitoring of global temperature trends from satellites', *Science,* Vol. 247, pp. 1,558-1,562.

Tegen, I., Lacis, A. A. and Fung, I. (1996): 'The influence on climate forcing of mineral aerosols from disturbed soils', *Nature,* Vol. 380, pp. 419-422.

Weber, G.R. (1996): 'Human effect on global climate?', *Nature,* Vol. 384, pp. 522-524.

2. Who Is Driving Climate Change Policy?

A winning coalition of advocacy: Climate Research, Bureaucracy and 'Alternative' Fuels [1]

Sonja Boehmer-Christiansen

Research bodies have long given unclear advice on climate change. A recent example from a German research body is the statement that there has been 'a shift in the consensus view of the experts in this field from predominantly doubtfully negative to predominantly doubtfully positive'. The doubt to which they refer is the human contribution to climatic change (not change as such).[2] This may be contrasted with statements made by politicians, which rarely exhibit such caution. Indeed, Tony Blair, Chancellor Kohl and President Clinton have all been quoted as saying that (human-induced) global warming is fact, not theory. Nevertheless, few governments have so far done much beyond what was economically attractive to them anyway. This paper considers what is going on.

Developing the Law of Climate Change: a Matter of Bureaucratic Sustainability

The subject of climate change remains poorly understood. Climate is an extremely complex set of phenomena that the physical and biological sciences are only beginning to explain. Hence there is considerable emphasis, in scientific publications, on uncertainty. This protects legitimate research interests, but has political implications.

Environmental bureaucracies and experts, as well as organised losers in the competitive world of fuel and energy technology supply, have a strong interest in man-made warming being true

---

[1] An earlier version of this paper appeared in *Energy Policy*, Vol. 25 (4), pp. 439 – 44.

[2] Klaus Hasselmann, MPI; from an open e-mail to the climate modelling community, June 1997.

and prefer that science comes to a consensus in their support. These three interest groups are supported by environmental non-governmental organisations (NGOs), which they have carefully cultivated since Rio.

As governments are the organisations that are called upon to implement mitigation strategies, they are the primary target of these 'green' pressures. However, because of their broad range of commitments and responsibilities, governments tend to be either unwilling or unable to deliver the policies that are demanded, which typically include increases in taxes on fossil fuels and subsidies to 'renewables', nuclear power, public transport and 'energy efficiency'. The World Bank and aid administrators are also called upon, by the same lobbies, to invest in 'cost-effective global environmental benefits', which typically means the 'transfer' (subsidised provision) of cleaner technologies and fuels to industrialising countries. A small range of projects is already being funded under the climate protection label by national and multilateral financial bodies, especially the Global Environment Facility (GEF). These projects and associated activities are enormously complex, requiring the acquisition and analysis of vast quantities of information. As a result, many experts in environmental and financial fields are employed to structure and oversee these projects. It is perhaps not surprising that these people have been amongst the strongest advocates of climate protection policy. Moreover, the World Bank and UN increasingly rely on such experts to justify policy interventions in client states, including 'Joint Implementation' (JI) projects that the GEF may be expected to fund in the future (Adams, 1996) but which so far have primarily attracted bilateral deals.

The above efforts are now underpinned by an international treaty, the Framework Convention on Climate Change (FCCC) and its associated institutions and networks. The third Conference of the Parties (CoP) of the FCCC meets this December in Kyoto and strenuous efforts to generate real commitments have been made. All the above-mentioned lobbies depend for their continued well-being on further progress being made in the definition of binding obligations under this treaty. These, in turn, hinge upon the existence of credible predictions of dangerous climate change at regional levels. Scientists, acting as experts serving political interests, deliver such predictions via summaries negotiated by the Intergovernmental Panel on Climate Change (IPCC). But can science, as a confirmed body of knowledge (and as distinct from the statements of scientists), do so?

The FCCC is the outcome of a complex process of global and national bargaining initiated in the mid-1980s by US-based research bodies. Ironically, these were at that time primarily motivated by a desire to protect nuclear power from the onslaughts of environmentalists. The objective of the FCCC as negotiated so far is the stabilisation of greenhouse gas concentrations 'at a level that would prevent dangerous anthropogenic interference with the climate system' (all treaty text cited from Churchill and Freestone, 1992, pp. 240-90). This, combined with the rider that stabilisation is to be achieved

'within a time frame sufficient to allow ecosystems to adapt naturally to climate change, to ensure that food supply is not threatened and to enable economic development to proceed in a sustainable manner',

remains inoperable until a stabilisation level is agreed, baselines and reduction targets are allocated to countries, and a great deal more is understood about the behaviour of ecosystems. Yet it is impossible to reach such agreements on scientific grounds. Not even global warming potentials can be derived from purely scientific criteria, no matter how politically desirable it would be to be able to aggregate the climate effects of the various greenhouse gases (Shackley and Wynne, 1997).

In spite of all this, the climate protection régime as developed so far has attracted considerable support. For this to be achieved, several ingredients were essential: science provided the threat, environmentalism provided emotion, rhetoric and the 'precautionary principle', new energy technologies promised greenhouse gas (GHG) emission reductions, and bureaucracies would provide the labour and intelligence needed to integrate all this into policy by drafting rational plans and devising clever strategies. Only then would politicians be required to provide the resources needed to translate the plan into action. We are about to reach this difficult stage; hence science is being revisited.

The FCCC was drafted by several networks of international experts working for a small number of governments. A close look at the hard substance of the FCCC reveals that its régime effectively codifies the research and data collection needs of the 'international scientific community' under the guidance of certain intergovernmental bureaucracies, which are in turn responsible for raising research funds and planning the global future (Boehmer-Christiansen, 1993). Economic development, land use and pollution control take place at the national level and cannot be dictated as easily, if at all, by intergovernmental treaties, although the making of plans may be required. Under the FCCC, reduction and mitigation plans are to be drawn up to:

'formulate, implement, publish and regularly update national and, where appropriate, regional programmes containing measures to mitigate climate change by addressing anthropogenic emissions by sources and removals by sinks of all greenhouse gases.... and measures to facilitate adequate adaptation to climate change; and promote and co-operate in the development, application and diffusion, including transfer, of technologies, practices and processes that control, reduce or prevent anthropogenic emissions' (FCCC Treaty, Article 4, paragraph 1b).

Resistance to such plans was to be expected and is now clearly observable, for the administrative loads alone are enormous. Governments are required to make inventories of all 'their' greenhouse gases using comparable methodologies and communicate these to the Conference of the Parties (CoP). Energy, transport, industry, forestry, waste management, coastal zone management, water resources, and agriculture impact assessment, as well as research collaboration, training and education, will need to be reported on.

However, as far as implementation goes, the treaty is a package held together, in logic, only as long as science lends credibility to the claim that human activities cause *controllable* net surface warming that is 'dangerous'. But who will define 'dangerous', what criteria will be used, and by whom will those criteria be selected? Will economic and political interests prevail (even if 'greenwashed' to persuade the gullible)? Before a definition can be agreed on the basis of sound science, vast quantities of data will be needed relating to the stabilisation of greenhouse gas (GHG) concentrations, the stabilisation of emissions, the definition of ecological limits or levels of tolerance to warming based on impact studies, and the methodologies for making national inventories of emissions and sinks.

So far, only the methodologies for greenhouse gas (GHG) inventories have been defined, with help from OECD and the Intergovernmental Panel on Climate Change (IPCC). Research bodies and administrations are collecting data sets and designing ambitious strategies that are of benefit to many institutions, especially those which tend to centralise control. Bureaucracies at all levels are being engaged in this enormous task. However, many countries are quite unable to comply without assistance. The GEF has therefore been called upon to fund such efforts under the label of 'capacity building' (in addition to its more conventional role of approving transfers of grants or loans for 'good quality', that is, World Bank- and CoP-approved projects). As a result, the FCCC has been described as a blank cheque for bureaucrats and indeed many of its negotiators have already gained handsomely from consultancies, prestigious UN or World Bank jobs, or access to the world of high politics. What has been overlooked by many, however, is the fact that in many poor countries more pressing national tasks have had to be postponed.

An Alliance Against 'Unsustainable' Coal Use

According to the FCCC, GHG emissions are to be stabilised by the year 2000. This is not a binding obligation and is unlikely to become one. Moreover, the Convention still does not specify what is to happen after 2000 and, although this is likely to be the primary focus of Kyoto, it seems unlikely that commitments will be as stringent as the 20 per cent reduction target proposed in Toronto in 1988, let alone the 60 per cent cut that is often demanded by environmentalists with reference to IPCC statements.[3] The CoP meetings of environment ministries in Berlin 1995 and Geneva 1996 may have taken these commitments a little further 'on paper', but treasuries and politicians remain reluctant to face the likely transition and compliance costs which would fall largely on energy industries and energy users. Australia, supported by Norway, is currently attempting to introduce the more sophisticated 'differentiated responsibility' concept, well known from the acid rain debate, to counter uniform percentage reduction targets.

Most efforts to limit GHG emissions would involve restrictions on the use of coal, especially in electricity generation. Indeed, such a policy is already being pursued by the GEF when funding projects on the basis of the costs per tonne of carbon dioxide removed.[4] Table 2.1 hints at the reasons for the attack on coal and at the motives of various energy players.

Table 2.1

Relative Carbon Dioxide Emission Factor Estimates for Different Fuels

Fuel	CO_2 Emission Factor
Natural gas*	15
Oil	18
Wood	19
Coal	25.3 (very variable)
Nuclear	0 (excluding construction & transport)

*Ignores efficiency of conversion or release of gas during transmission. The thermal efficiency of coal-fired plant has increased from 25 per cent to 38 per cent since the 1950s; that of combined cycle gas plant is approaching 50 per cent, while gas burned directly has of course a much higher efficiency.

Source: OECD (1991)

---

[3] An attempt by NGOs to get agreement on a higher percentage was opposed by the nuclear research lobby. For example, Wolfgang Hafele is reported to have argued that the timetable was too tight for the adoption of breeder reactors.

[4] The GEF has largely resisted supporting clean coal technologies, although there are a few exceptions, such as China.

The attack on coal can be explained by non-environmental motives. Rising oil prices during the 1970s had created new winners in the world of energy supply and R&D: more efficient technologies, nuclear power and renewables. Gas was not yet available for electricity generation and energy demand was expected to rise steeply, a development that has become fact only in parts of the developing world. During this period, energy suppliers were not attracted to climate change, though the issue was already being debated in research circles (Kellogg and Schware, 1981) and members of some national bureaucracies noted an opportunity for expansion of their role.[5] The market did not yet need an ally in environmentalism — prices alone were moving energy options away from low tech fossil fuels towards the options advocated in response to the 'energy crisis': nuclear power, 'renewables', and gas exploration. When fossil fuel prices began to fall again in the mid-1980s (and they fell especially sharply in 1986), the situation reversed and the newcomers sought a green ally. Powerful commercial incentives began to operate to demand official measures to maintain the competitiveness of 'clean' energy in the name of 'sustainability'. The IPCC was conceptualised in 1985, planned in 1987 and began operating in 1988.

By the mid-1980s, non-fossil energy interests and several major governments strongly committed to new technologies and fuels because of sunk investments, felt sufficiently threatened to pay attention to environmentalists and scientists disseminating worst case scenarios: the global hothouse, floods and hurricanes. However, stagnant demand and falling prices are not an easy context for governments to subsidise higher cost energy options. Further research to reduce uncertainties seemed more attractive and extant scientific knowledge appeared to justify that. Moreover, some emissions reductions were being achieved through the transition to natural gas (which also boosted the revenue of certain oil companies and countries). So the main economic losers (nuclear, 'renewables', 'energy efficiency' technologies) began to look for help to the well-prepared

---

[5] The interests of the British senior civil service in the Foreign Office date back to this period.

environmental lobby. Fossil fuel interests, the villains of the piece according to those who subscribe to the man-made global warming story, replied in kind, turning to scientific uncertainty for support but pointing to population growth and China's rising energy demand or consumption by the rich as the real culprits.

Yet intervention was not as readily forthcoming as had once been hoped for, or feared. Fossil fuel prices were too low. Many countries will fail to stabilise their carbon dioxide emissions by 2000.[6] While this gas can now be removed from plumes, and R&D concerned with carbon dioxide fixation and 'zero emission power generation' is booming in technologically advanced countries, subsequent containment is only economically feasible where CO_2 is not a pure waste product.[7] Technology promises much but, as is so often the case, the constraints will not be technical but economic and political. Reducing GHG emissions per unit of energy generated is feasible over time but, because of energy demand growth, this is not likely to deliver overall reductions of the nature apparently needed to stabilise concentrations at predictable levels.

The observable climate strategies of several governments are therefore better explained not as responses to environmental pressure, but as 'side effects' of their energy policies or energy demand developments. 'Activist' countries usually have energy policy interests which 'naturally' converge with emission reduction. For example, Britain could not have waxed in support of 'precaution' had not privatised industry been forced into price competition and therefore delivered emissions reductions by fuel switching, and had not the Treasury agreed to subsidise nuclear power for political reasons. Many UK coal-fired power stations were closed in the early 1990s and more are likely to follow for purely commercial reasons. The 'cleanest' option for 2000, it has

---

6   German compliance so far is the result of East Germany's industrial collapse. In the UK the 'dash to gas' ensured compliance with economic and political benefits. Human costs are ignored.

7   Norway is a world leader in the injection of carbon dioxide into sandstone under the North Sea. CO_2 is a by-product of the gas export industry: Norwegian gas contains 9 per cent carbon dioxide, which has to be reduced to 2.5 per cent before the gas can be sold. Removal is essential for commercial reasons, whilst containment off-shore is mandated in order to stabilise emissions.

been shown for the UK, would be a mix of only gas and uranium, which is also likely to be the cheapest, at least in the short run.[8]

German emissions limits have been achieved primarily because of the industrial collapse of eastern Germany and the same is true for the countries which once formed the USSR. We can see that governments support GHG emission targets for a variety of non-environmental reasons: to strengthen national nuclear industries (e.g. Germany), to enhance export potentials for gas or nuclear electricity (e.g. France and Norway), or to attract aid flows. The EC attempted to use the issue to strengthen its own competence by trying to introduce a Community tax through the back door.

Economies heavily dependent on coal for electricity generation face the most serious difficulties if required to reduce emissions rapidly, and have therefore been noted to be among the most sceptical about global warming, even though technologically advanced importers of oil or coal may be sympathetic to a degree of emission control in order to encourage energy efficiency or to promote advanced energy technologies, such as Japan and Germany. The Bush administration's refusal to accept stronger commitments is said to have stemmed from the wish to protect oil and coal interests. The change in attitude by the Clinton administration was probably related more to pro-gas changes in US energy legislation, an approaching election and declining reliance on coal than to new scientific understanding. Expected benefits from Joint Implementation (JI) in Eastern Europe and Russia are likely to be decisive in future. As the USA became less willing to defend fossil fuel interests, Australia as a major coal exporter has come to adopt this role. With no nuclear power and little gas, the Australian green vote was too small to keep the discredited Labour government in power.

To industrialising countries such as China the whole issue is primarily one of attracting cheaper money into their infrastructure developments. In 1992, the World Bank argued that world use and production of energy 'can only be changed

---

[8] In the daily bidding system, electricity from coal-fired power stations fitted with FGD can no longer compete with subsidised gas and nuclear power for the base load. Hence, current attempts to import 'petcoke' from the USA to dilute local coal.

marginally in the next thirty years' because of 'weak administrative and institutional structures' (World Energy Council, 1993, p.20). This was clearly an invitation for 'capacity building' and joint implementation projects which the Bank is now actively pursuing, although serious power struggles continue over who precisely is to define the criteria for the use of international funds available for the implementation of the climate treaty.

A great deal of economic and political activity concerned with 'energy' is therefore justified with reference to 'science', or rather to threats which are claimed to be predicted by science. One may therefore wonder how the international institutions of science managed to raise and sustain the global warming threat in the first place? In the early 1970s there had been the threat of cooling, a possibility discussed at the 1972 UN Stockholm Conference on Environment and Human Development with reference to aerosols and especially dust particles; but this scenario was of very little interest to the energy world.

Earth Systems Research — Underpinning Science Advice

The early efforts of the natural science research community, including the famous Villach meetings of the mid-1980s, are described elsewhere (Boehmer-Christiansen, 1994, 1996). Here, only the attractions of climate change to scientific bureaucracies are summarised. Climate change now constitutes a key label for very large 'policy-relevant' or 'strategic' research packages involving significant amounts of administrative supervision and assessment by bureaucracies ranging from the OECD and the EU to most UN agencies and national research councils. The IPCC fits into this network as the body which best represents the interests of science in government, or directly funded by it. In the fields concerned, this covers most scientific research. Global modelling and earth observation, the tools of climate research, are 'big' science and take place largely outside universities. Their financial foundations are precarious because they tend to be directly dependent on political good will.

The World Meteorological Organisation's (WMO) interest in climate change research dates back to the mid-1970s, when its

Climate Panel recommended a research programme on the subject, although even in 1979 delegates to the WMO, especially those from Britain and America, remained doubtful whether climate (as opposed simply to 'weather') should become a major focus for WMO administered research. However, by 1981 a World Climate Research Programme (WCRP) was underway, albeit short of funding. It soon became a major part of the 'global change' research agenda which aims to model the physical Earth, including land use and emissions (WMO, 1986). In this effort WCRP supplements the International Geosphere Biosphere Programme (IGBP),[9] as well as research on environmental monitoring and climate impacts undertaken under the auspices of the United Nations Environment Programme (UNEP). The IGBP is now being implemented with the support of a number of national secretariats in the major research nations, UNEP, WCRP and UNESCO's oceanographic programmes. Further stages are planned. Behind these intergovernmental institutions is the International Council for Scientific Unions (ICSU), the scientific bureaucracy of academic natural science. The IGBP System for Training, Analysis, Research and Training (START) programme is aimed at strengthening the scientific capacity of poor countries and is assisted by the GEF. Links between IPCC and IGBP, and national research bodies, can be demonstrated by cross-membership of senior research managers and scientists.

All the above programmes were heavily influenced if not designed by US science administrators in the early 1980s. While the pure objective is the full understanding of the physical systems of the planet Earth, including the impacts of the human species as first envisaged by American scientists in the 1950s, the US agenda was written as 'a step in the evolving process of defining the scientific needs for understanding changes in the global environment, changes that are of great concern' (US

---

[9] IGBP builds on collaborations between atmospheric scientists which date back to the 1950s, e.g. the Global Atmospheric Research Programme managed by Bert Bolin, until recently chairman of the full IPCC, as well as UNESCO's Man and Biosphere Programme.

National Research Council, 1990).[10] It was disseminated globally for approval and implementation by ICSU in response to a concern that the climate threat had so miraculously created. The research is primarily defined by and for those working in the natural sciences and will take another decade or so to complete. Achieving its objective will involve more attention to complex biotic feedbacks often heavily influenced by human activity, such as land-use changes, and also to ocean circulation, the hydrological and the carbon cycles, as well as to 'socio-economic' assumptions of the emissions scenarios fed into the physical system. The economisation of nature and human nature is being promoted by this research agenda through the use of global models to forecast the impact of economic regulations, such as taxes, on world GNP and speculation about the costs and benefits of both global warming and its mitigation in dollar terms. However, in general economists have been more careful than some natural scientists, including leading IPCC figures, in advocating energy policy on the basis of their theoretical findings.

The Functioning of the IPCC

The IPCC emerged in 1988 from inside the WMO with the help of UNEP and ICSU research networks. It periodically releases ambivalent summaries specifically addressed to policy-makers, as well as long scientific summaries addressed primarily to the scientific community. Only the former are read outside the scientific community and have attracted attention and resources to international research programmes. The latter serve to focus the research carried out under these programmes and thereby help to ensure that subsequent findings follow the general pattern.

The IPCC stresses available technical solutions and its famous 'scientific consensus' is designed by scientists and government

---

[10] In 1990 the US Committee on Global Change and the US National Committee for the IGBP of the National Research Council published a report developed between 1986 and 1988 which became the foundation for the IGBP. The original idea, 'Towards an International Geosphere-Biosphere Program: A Study of Global Change', was published in 1983. Its implementation was recommended by the 1985 Villach Conference, when the WCRP was recommended to governments.

officials joined by common interests to keep the ship afloat. The underlying IPCC promise to politicians is that climate change is sufficiently predictable and will eventually allow rational decision-making at the global level. In theory this may be true.

The individuals on the IPCC governing body primarily represent the interests of natural science research, although recently some mainstream economic modellers have been added. IPCC working groups have paid little attention to why governments might find the implementation of technical options for reducing emissions difficult or even impossible. Politics and the need for understanding society, as distinct from collecting socio-economic data, were largely excluded from earlier deliberations. Research relevant to the IPCC concerns subjects that political leaders considered 'safe': technical matters, such as the diagnosis of future environmental problems, were to be explored with the aid of the latest developments in space and information technology. Much of the research upon which the IPCC draws is directly funded by government and prescribed by environment ministries.

The IPCC governing body consists of a small secretariat and bureau of about 50 people, with the former based inside the WMO in Geneva. The plenary body brings together leading government scientists and research managers with diplomats and government officials. The bureau is the facilitator of consensus and originator of policy-makers' summaries which are released to the media and the world of politics. The scientific work of the Panel takes place under the supervision of approved scientists whose main task is to co-ordinate the reports of working groups and attract funding for underpinning national research; the IPCC itself does not do research or fund it. The former NASA ozone scientist and chairman of one IPCC working group (WG), Robert Watson, has also acted as adviser to the US President and is currently an employee of the World Bank. He has recently replaced Professor Bert Bolin as chair of the full IPCC, illustrating the fusion of science and government in the IPCC.

The collection and writing up of information is in the hands of selected lead authors in charge of a large number of subgroups of three (original) working groups – WGI, WGII and WGIII – covering science, impacts and responses respectively. WGs I and

II reflected the existing research interests of WMO and UNEP respectively. WGIII served the needs of governments more directly, allowing officials to meet policy advocates from NGOs and industry.[11] It remains the responsibility of each WG to gather and evaluate 'sound', i.e. trusted, knowledge and draw advice from it. The next report is due in 2000, and work schedules have already been defined. Science is to be 'discovered' according to politically defined schedules.

For example, WG I gathers and assesses available scientific information on climate change science. Its co-chairman remains Sir John Houghton, a British meteorologist with strong religious views and a long career as a government advisor.[12] Only his group was able to base itself, in 1987, on a well-established research network and close links with large climate research institutions in North America, the then USSR[13] and Germany (Max Planck Institutes), as well as national meteorological offices. This group is still working effectively from a small secretariat within the Hadley Centre for Climate Prediction and Research in the UK, partly funded by the UK Department of the Environment (DoE) and using the MET Office research facilities

---

[11] WGs II and III were merged in 1994 and a third group on 'cross-cutting', i.e. socio-economic, issues was set up. In 1995, this group became enmeshed in controversy over statistical estimates of the value of life as part of its efforts to cost climate change damage.

[12] Sir John accepted this post when he was permanent UK representative to WMO on the condition that the UK government provided sufficient resources. As a former director of the UK Met Office, following a career in space and atmospheric physics, he was extremely well placed to link national bodies to international ones. As chairman of the Royal Commission on Environmental Pollution and member of the UK Government's Panel on Sustainable Development he has defended the IPCC on various occasions against attacks from other disciplines which want excluded areas of knowledge examined more closely, such as the roles of hydrology, solar forces, carbon dioxide chemistry, and the impact of aerosols, such as minerals and carbon particles, not included in current models. See *Nature*, 6 April 1996, for suggestions that the net effect of human activities over large areas may be cooling.

[13] The Russians have been badly treated inside the IPCC, in part because of methodological differences (weak modelling capacity), in part because they have remained sceptics (on scientific grounds, e.g. Kirill Kondratyev who believes that the IPCC, by ignoring the complex effects of aerosols and weak observational inputs, has greatly exaggerated the 'danger' of warming) or supported warming on the grounds that this would benefit mankind.

and observational data funded by the DoE (Boehmer-Christiansen, 1995). The IPCC structure reveals a highly linear model of policy process in which 'science' thinks and recommends in isolation from society, while politicians accept and implement the facts and uncertainties. This model is unrealistic because it ignores politics and does not admit to the uncertainties of science. The assumption (known as the 'Enlightenment Fallacy') that knowledge automatically produces response is accepted without question (Berry, 1993, p.314). This serves the interests of science (or at least certain sections of the scientific establishment, which benefit from increased funding). The British political class also benefits from its support of the IPCC because of the opportunities this offers to pursue low-cost UN environmental diplomacy and to transfer of information, capacity and technology to the 'South' (with all the attendant voter appeal of such politically correct actions).

Policy Advice from Science and the Politicisation of the IPCC

Recent warming predictions made in the UK have declined significantly (Mason, 1996),[14] though one would hardly think so on the basis of political announcements, press reports, even IPCC statements as reported by the UN (DoE, 1996; press statements, June 1997).[15] Few have dared to challenge the science underlying

---

[14] In a lecture given at the University of Hull in November 1996, Sir John Mason made it quite clear that he considered population growth and not climate change the most significant global problem, pointing out the significant decline in the predicted average warming and the large uncertainties surrounding aerosols. The average warming range predicted per decade in 1990 was 0.3°C for a doubling of carbon dioxide, today it is 0.2°C per decade, with the German model, reportedly to the displeasure of government, giving an even lower figure. Large uncertainties remain as many factors cannot be included for lack of scientific understanding.

[15] A former Secretary of State for the Environment, Mr John Gummer pressed for urgent precautionary action by exaggerating the IPCC conclusions and by linking an IPCC phrase to his own, i.e. 'discernible human influence on the climate mainly as a result of greenhouse gas emissions from burning fossil fuels...'. The IPCC carefully avoids making such a link. Even DoE civil servants are more cautious, claiming merely that the observed small increase in surface temperature since the late 19th century is a change 'unlikely to be entirely natural in origin'. How much of this increase is the result of humankind's actions is of course the essence of the policy response problem. The new government, under Tony Blair, appears to have adopted the Gummer

even moderate warming prediction (Emsley, 1996), although even the famous scientific consensus has recently been described as 'limited' in a scientific journal (Houghton, 1996, p. 572).

Global warming believers usually argue that the IPCC at last confirmed the need for mitigation action in 1995. Closer examination confirms that previous ambiguities continue. In March 1995 it was agreed that:

'...This qualitative evidence does not prove conclusively that a cause and effect relationship exists between anthropogenic activities and the response of the climate system, nor does it allow us to quantify the magnitude of the effect. However, the best evidence that we have at present, drawn together from quantitative studies and qualitative sources, indicates that human activities have had an identifiable effect on climate' (Callender, 1996, Appendix).

Note that the claim is not 'climate change' or even warming, but simply climate.

By November 1995, after intense debate and several other formulations, this became the better known:

'Our ability to quantify the human influence on global climate is currently limited because the expected signal is still emerging from the noise of natural variability, and because there are uncertainties in key factors. These include the magnitude and patterns of long term natural variability and the time-evolving pattern of forcing by, and response to, changes in the concentrations of greenhouse gases and aerosols, and land surface changes. Nevertheless, the balance of evidence suggests that there is a discernible human influence on global climate' (*ibid.*).

By what criteria was the evidence 'balanced'? Advocates may still select between two positions, which may be contrasted with the 1990 IPCC Science Report. This predicted 'with certainty' a rate of increase of global mean temperature during the next century of about 0.3°C per decade '[which] will result in a likely

---

position to the full for what appear to be reasons linked less to diplomacy than as a justification for increasing taxes on petrol.

increase in global mean temperature of about 1°C above the present value by *2025*' (Houghton *et al.*, 1990, p.11). Certainty apparently created in one phrase, by the use of 'will', is taken away in another, by the use of 'likely'.

As far as 'closed' science understanding is concerned, a view made in 1987 that '...the range of scientific uncertainty is currently so large that neither "do nothing" nor "prevent emissions" can be excluded from consideration' (Warrick and Jones, 1988, p. 62), surely still holds today for reasons to be mentioned below. The two authors pleaded in the late 1980s that it was imperative to extend full support to a two-pronged research effort that would narrow the range of scientific uncertainty regarding the greenhouse effect, while identifying and defining ways in which socio-economic and environmental systems were likely to be affected. This early plea completely ignored two research areas, solutions and adaptation, which have since been battling to be included in the research agenda.

The impact of research agendas on policy raises major questions about the nature and funding of contemporary, government-funded science with its short-term contracts and the myopia inherent to political decision-making. Natural science appears to promote itself increasingly with reference to environmental threats, which it promises to be able to measure and predict. The reduction of uncertainties is then linked to cost savings and competitiveness, the mantra of contemporary politics and business. If 'big' research plays its cards right, it may be allowed to research climate change for another decade or so. It will continue to predict warming by relatively simple mathematical computations that are easily manipulated. The activities of the scientific community and the IPCC as suppliers of information to environmental administrations are therefore of significance in any explanation of climate policy.

Conclusions

Scientific advice derived at the frontiers of research is by nature inconclusive. Research thrives on debate and controversy, not on consensus. The political weakness of science that is funded to be consensual and policy-relevant tends to bring forth advice that is ambiguous because it strives to serve all parties. In the end, scientists may become unwilling to involve themselves in policy debates (Proctor, 1991). Climate change politics so far have largely created proposals and data that have transformed the noble goal of protecting the global atmosphere into a utilitarian game about regulatory intervention and planning at a time when governments were trying to escape such public responsibilities. The 'South' may be the first victim, or beneficiary, of this development.

Climate policy cannot be understood without a more sophisticated view of the role of science and a better understanding of the coalition of non-environmental interests, both commercial and bureaucratic, which now drives the issue internationally. Where this coalition will take us is still not clear.

References

Adams, D. (1996): 'Joint Implementation: Opportunities for business under the UN Framework Convention on Climate Change', London: FT Energy Publishing.

Boehmer-Christiansen, S. A. (1993): 'Scientific Consensus and Climate Change: the codification of a global research agenda', *Energy and Environment*, 4(4) pp. 362-406. See also in IPCC-related papers in *Global Environmental Change* (1994) 4 (2 and 3); in *Environmental Politics* (1995), 4 (1 and 2).

Boehmer-Christiansen, S. A. (1996): 'Political pressures in the formation of scientific consensus', in Emsley (1996).

Berry, S. (1993): 'Green religion and green science', *RSA Journal*, Vol. CXLI, No. 5438, April.

Callender, B. (1996): 'Global climatic change – the latest scientific understanding', draft paper presented to the 28th International Geographical Congress, The Hague, Netherlands, 4-10 August 1996 (mimeo).

Churchill, S. and Freestone, D. (eds.) (1992): *International Law and Climate Change*, London: Graham and Trotman/Nijhoff.

Department of the Environment (1996): *Climate Change Briefing*, London, October.

Emsley, J. (ed.) (1996): *The Global Warming Debate*, London: European Science and Environment Forum.

Houghton, J. T., Jenkins, G. J. and Ephraums, J. J. (1990): *Climate Change – The IPCC Scientific Assessment*, Intergovernmental Panel on Climate Change, Cambridge: Cambridge University Press.

Houghton, J. T. (1996): Letter, *Nature*, Vol. 384, p. 572.

Kellogg, W. W. and Schware, R. (eds.) (1981): *Climate Change and Society: Consequences of Increasing Carbon Dioxide*, Michigan: Westview Press.

Mason, B. J. (1996): 'Predictions of climate changes caused by man-made emission of greenhouse gases: a critical assessment', *Contemporary Physics*, Vol. 36(5), pp. 299-319.

Proctor, R. (1991): *Value Free Science? Purity and Power in Modern Knowledge*, Cambridge, Mass.: Harvard University Press.

Shackley, S. and Wynne, B. (1997): 'Global Warming Potentials: ambiguity or precision as an aid to policy?', *Climate Research*, Vol. 8, pp. 89-107.

US National Research Council (1990): *Research Strategies for the US Global Change Research Program*, Washington DC: National Academy Press.

Warrick, R. A. and Jones, P. D. (1988): 'The Greenhouse Effect: Impacts and Policies', *Forum for Applied Research and Public Policy*, Fall, pp. 44-62.

WEC (1993): *World Energy Council Journal*, July.

World Meteorological Organisation (1986): *Report of the International Conference on the assessment of carbon dioxide and other greenhouse gases in climate variations and associated impacts*, Villach, 9-15 October 1985, WMO Nn. 661, Geneva.

Young, Z. and Boehmer-Christiansen, S. A. (1997): 'Investing in the planet: opportunities and risks in getting money from the GEF', *Power Economics*, Vol. 1(3), pp. 40-43.

3. The Politicisation of Climate Science

Roger Bate

The general public seems to believe that the climate is changing due to human activities. They hear from environmental groups and the media that those changes will be harmful and that we should be doing something about it. However, within the scientific community things are not so clear-cut. Existing scientific evidence does not support the call for urgent action and the conventional wisdom concerning climate science is based on a false notion of scientific consensus. While the media deserve to take some blame for common misperceptions, they are only partially responsible. The scientists, or more accurately those in the science bureaucracy, are more culpable. In the climate change debate, political and economic pressures have corrupted the scientific process. This paper posits an explanation as to why this has occurred.

Corrupted Science

Science is a discovery process in which hypotheses are put forward, tested through empirical research and the gathering of data, and then revised to reflect the findings. Corrupted science, however, is science that does not move from hypothesis to data to conclusion, but from mandated or politically acceptable conclusion back to selected data in order to reach the mandated or acceptable conclusion. It is a reverse and perverse methodology, in which the right answers are known before the right questions are asked.

Corrupted science not only misrepresents the true state of knowledge, but also the scientific process itself. The selectivity of its process is denied and dissenting perspectives are excluded due to the need for 'approved' conclusions. There is little doubt that this tendency is extremely dangerous, for it undermines the scientific process and threatens the ability of science to provide insights and answers about the world around us. Insofar as science becomes a tool for political agendas, its value as a social institution is diminished.

The Model of the Future

Climate science is about the future and what will happen there, so that is where my discussion begins.

Any successful strategist, from a chess player to a world leader, will think ahead, use 'what if' scenarios, and second-guess others' reactions or feedback. In short, we seek to plan for the events that lie ahead. Thus scientists and other academics seek to develop models of the future to address the need to know what lies ahead.

Economics, for example, has great analytical value where inputs are known, or can be reasonably estimated. But to try to produce a definitive socio-economic forecast is tricky. Making bold predictions about future trends when even the direction of change is unknown can only damage the credibility of the discipline in the long run. Thus, economists give best and worst case scenarios, and lay out their premises – some of which they know may be wrong – and acknowledge their uncertainties. Were they to do otherwise, uncertainties would become assumptions, which would be used as a basis for economic computer models, which produce concise answers that look authoritative. The basic assumptions would inevitably be forgotten and the answers swallowed whole without the required amount of salt.

Most climate modellers have followed a similar course, making predictions with the requisite caveats and underlining the uncertainties. Others have not been so circumspect, which is exactly how the global warming scare started. The level of uncertainty in climate science is such that it is unable to predict even the direction, let alone the magnitude, of a physical change. Scientists still do not know much about feedback mechanisms within the climate, and the myriad variables they can affect.

Take the example of regional rainfall. Primitive computer models of the mid-1980s predicted metres of inundation coinciding with whole degrees of temperature rise. The picture was of a climate catastrophe. Yet with every improvement in modelling technique, these predictions have become more modest: metres have become centimetres; degrees, 10ths of degrees; and so on. The models are still not up to the job of 'simulating' past weather, but the genie is out of the bottle. Global warming is a political issue and thus has a life of its own, outside and beyond science. Climate change, as we must call it, has become a juggernaut, both in the policy process and in the scientific community as well.

Look to Motives

Despite the shortcomings of economic forecasting – economic trends as uncertain as climatic trends – there is a branch of economics that offers insight into the climate change debate. 'Public choice' theory explains why the incentives faced by scientists, politicians, pressure groups and businessmen are important to the political dynamic on a given issue. Although these incentives are often ignored by policy-makers and economists, their inclusion in the analysis of public choices has been justified by the work of, amongst others, Nobel prize-winners James Buchanan and George Stigler. Public choice theory provides important insights into the actions of all the players in the climate debate; I have documented this analysis elsewhere (Bate, 1996).

Conventional wisdom has it that public servants apply their professional training and expertise in the public interest and not in their own; that government works on behalf of the people for the people. Public choice theorists argue that this view is naïve. They examine the individuals involved in the making and executing of public policies and the incentives they face. It turns out that most people, most of the time, find it impossible to argue against their own interests. The bottom line is that bureaucrats, like just about everyone else, respond to the incentives they face and mostly do what they perceive to be best for them and their nearest and dearest.

The public choice model of political decision-making divides society into four groups: voters, politicians, bureaucrats and interest groups. Each actor is assumed to want something from the system: voters want better government, politicians want votes, bureaucrats want job security and enlarged budgets, interest groups want income. Politicians, bureaucrats and interest groups have distinct advantages over the voters. They are

75

professionals who typically know more about their specialist subject than does the average voter (partly because voters remain rationally ignorant of most policy issues – that is, the benefits of gathering information are expected to be less than the costs). The global warming issue involves all these actors, vying in a game of competing interests.

According to economists Mitchell and Simmons, politicians and public figures

'find it highly rational to engage in obfuscation, play-acting, myth-making ritual, the suppression and distortion of information, stimulation of hatred and envy, and the promotion of excessive hopes' (Mitchell and Simmons, 1994, pp. 63-64).

Climate Interest Groups

The various groups acting in the climate change debate result in a political process driven by perverse incentives. Climate change could affect everyone. However, most individuals are not, nor can they be, directly involved in the policy debate, so they remain rationally ignorant of the facts. Those with a direct interest in the debate include energy suppliers, sectors that are indirectly affected (such as insurance, banking and transport), those whose business is the protection of the natural environment, and those with more subtle incentives. These last include the scientists, the science-led bureaucracies and the political entrepreneurs; they are treated less critically by the media, and as a result their credibility is enhanced, although their interests are not necessarily any more pure.

The incentives faced by businessmen are fairly apparent. Solar power and nuclear power executives want climate change to be real because their businesses would proliferate as fossil fuel-based electricity suppliers are forced to reduce emissions. For the same reason, oil and coal executives hope talk of climate change is nothing but hot air. Other businessmen have mixed incentives but most would prefer it if climate change is not being caused by man, since they would also suffer under increased regulatory intervention – *viz.* the strong public stance taken by the CEOs of the American Business Roundtable against a climate treaty.

Similarly, green pressure groups can gain kudos and funding for promoting climate change. Nothing raises money like crisis and the consequent publicity. As US Interior Secretary Bruce Babbitt, himself the former head of the League of Conservation Voters, remarked, 'The bottom line for environmentalists is how do you induce people to send money to sustain the movement' (Adler, 1995, p. xxii; see also the discussion therein on the falling fortunes of environmental organisations). Thus, environmental groups issue direct mail appeals and take out advertisements hyping fears of a greenhouse catastrophe, demonstrating the need for their continued vigilance. After all, if there is no environmental crisis, what need do people have for Greenpeace?

Politicians also have much to gain. Facing credibility problems at home they seek to become statesmen in the international arena – an arena in which they are less accountable for their actions. They can sign treaties that their citizens have heard little about and that will not take effect for years to come, after the political leaders are safely out of office. Those politicians fortunate enough to be representing countries that will meet their targets can score additional green points from acting in their national interest anyway. Many mistakenly believe global trade to be a zero sum game, and that by demanding urgent action on global warming from other countries they will benefit at home where measures are not yet in place. Thus, at the July United Nations 'Rio plus 5' summit in New York, British Prime Minister Tony Blair and German Chancellor Helmut Kohl admonished the US for its energy profligacy. What remained left unsaid was that the UK and Germany would meet their year-2000 emission reduction targets because of non-environmental factors. Lower carbon dioxide emissions in the UK have more to do with the transition to gas-fired power stations, due to Margaret Thatcher's energy market liberalisation, whilst lower emissions in Germany are more the result of the failure of the East German coal industry than of any environmental leadership in Europe.

The above incentives seem evident and are perhaps close to conventional wisdom (few people raise an eyebrow when you suggest that industry acts in its own interests, whilst the plethora of scandals in recent years has opened up the public's eye to the

77

(potential for political corruptibility). Academics, however, have generally remained above suspicion, especially in Europe. Why is this? 'Objectivity' in science comes from open debate, credibility comes from peer-review. Scientists' integrity rests on this debate and peer-review process. Anything that damages these precious qualities threatens the public's trust in science's pronouncements. One would therefore assume that scientists would be relatively immune to public choice pressures, and they may be less subject to such incentives than other groups, but they are still human nonetheless.

Climate change involves myriad scientific disciplines but is dominated by just a few, the most important being dynamic mathematical modelling. Not because it is more important to knowledge than other sciences, but because it is the one discipline that purports to provide the vision of the future wanted by the media – and the political system.

Unlike international trade, short-run government science funding is often a zero-sum game. Determining who gets what slice of the pie is a decision based upon many criteria, including political relevance of the science. There is no doubt that dynamic modelling can be more relevant to policy than paleobotany and it has received the lion's share of climate funding in recent years – at the expense of other disciplines, increased overall funding notwithstanding. There is only so much research money to go around.

Scientists must be aware of this fact. If there is less need for their discipline or their research, there will be less money to fund their endeavours. The Hadley Centre at the UK Meteorological Office exists largely because of climate change and the money it brings in. If climate change were suddenly to disappear as an issue, Hadley might even close, with its $20 million annual budget allocated to other research. The Max Planck Institute in Germany and the University of East Anglia in the UK are two other major European research centres that have benefited from the climate change debate.

Scientists lucky enough to be in disciplines related to global warming (and there are lots of them), have benefited greatly in the last 10 years, much to the chagrin of scientists in less fashionable fields whose work may well be of more immediate and certain importance. More is spent on climate research in the UK than is spent on cancer research, for example. So, those at the mercy of the fickle funder are wise to keep doubts to themselves.

In short, big science, including the development and running of big computer models, requires big money. Competition for funding is intense. In this environment, publicity and 'policy relevance' help in the scramble for funds – climate change has both. Due to their success in capturing funding many climate scientists' careers now depend on global warming. As Dr Matt Ridley, writing in the *Sunday Telegraph*, put it:

'Imagine that you have been toiling away at atmospheric physics for 30 years and suddenly along comes global warming. Next thing you know the United Nations is paying you hundreds of pounds a day to sit in Madrid sampling room service and appearing on Newsnight. Would you admit that the whole thing was nothing to worry about?' (Ridley, 1995)

So scientists, along with business and political players (and the media, another interest group that merits a discussion of its own), have an interest in how information about climate change is presented. In such an environment, formal scientific procedures and peer review become that much more important, and deviations from accepted procedural norms become inherently suspect.

Peer Review Problems

The issue of peer review itself is an important one, which shows the biases inherent in modern science. Scientists often blame the media for exaggerating stories of alarm, but of course it is not just the media that like exciting 'positive' results. Scientific journals like the attention that publication of exciting or ground-breaking research can bring.

A recent paper in the science journal *Oikos* explained how research which is important, but not exciting or innovative, seldom makes it into the more prestigious scientific journals. Those journals rarely carry papers where the findings are largely 'negative'. For example, a researcher might analyse the data relating to the link between pesticide residues in apples and bladder cancer, and conclude that his results indicated no correlation. One would think that the information discovered by the researcher would be useful for those working in similar fields. But the results are not exciting, and the chance of the paper being published in a top journal like *Nature* is remote. To come to this conclusion, the study's authors analysed 1,812 scientific papers published between 1989 and 1995 picked at random from 40 biology journals. Only 9 per cent of the papers contained 'non-significant' results; the figure was even lower for the most prestigious journals (Csada *et al.*, 1996, p. 591).

Given the pressure on university researchers to publish – and in good journals – the bias against publishing 'negative' results has some worrying implications. First, it is likely that the hypotheses to be tested will be conservative, because positive results will seem more likely in such cases. More outlandish hypotheses –ones that might broaden the scientific picture – will not be entertained. Second, researchers are likely to select carefully the data in search of a significant correlation. If the chance of being published is increased by showing a positive result, researchers will be tempted to trawl through the data until they find one – ignoring all the negative correlations they encounter on the way. Careers may depend on such things.

So while the media want alarming or positive-result stories, so do the best journals. Saying that an ice-shelf has become larger, that tree lines and temperatures were higher in the past, or that uncertainties remain, is simply not good enough to attract attention to one's research. Is it any wonder that university refutations of the man-made-climate-change thesis are so rare? A fair representation of the peer-reviewed literature would therefore be biased in favour of man-made global warming, so there is even less need to fiddle with reports.

Climate Consensus?

Prompted by funding applications from US climate modellers in the late 1970s, two United Nations bodies, the World Meteorological Organisation (WMO) and the UN Environment Programme (UNEP), embraced climate research. In 1988, as global warming was fast becoming a prominent issue, these two bodies set up the Intergovernmental Panel on Climate Change (IPCC) as a 'mechanism aimed at providing the basis for the development of a realistic and effective internationally accepted strategy for addressing climate change'. It may be significant that even then there was an underlying assumption that 'climate change' was a given that needed to be 'addressed' by international action.

With its assumptions in hand, the machine trundled on, commissioning research, holding international meetings in exotic locations and producing a series of reports on the state of climate science and various policy options. The hallmark of these reports, according to Richard Lindzen, Professor of Meteorology at the Massachusetts Institute of Technology, was 'waffle statements which don't say anything, which nobody can disagree with' (Wilkie, 1995).

Things changed with the IPCC's Second Assessment Report in 1995. It stated that '[t]he balance of the evidence suggests that there is a discernible human influence on global climate'. This statement was seized upon by environmental interest groups and the press as final evidence of a scientific consensus on climate change. Environmental leaders pronounced it definitive proof that urgent action was warranted. But was the 'scientific consensus' supporting this view politically engineered? The contributing scientists themselves were expressing quiet uncertainty.

The credibility of the source of scientific information is important. Most commentators assume that scientific documents are based on science, not politics, and hence are objective. The IPCC is seen as providing a politically relevant consensus view, in part because it relies upon the scientific peer-review process. Everything is read, discussed, modified and approved by a panel of experts. Its reputation hangs on this critical approach and its adherence to strict governmental review procedures. But as one IPCC lead author, Dr Keith Shine of Reading University, described the process of producing the IPCC Policymakers summary:

'We produce a draft, and then the policymakers go through it line by line and change the way it is presented. ... They don't change the data, but the way it's represented. It is peculiar that they have the final say in what goes into a scientists' report' (Winton, 1995).

The science is scientific, but the spin placed upon it is political (Grubb, 1996).

The main report approved by the world's governments at the IPCC plenary in Madrid in 1995, but not published until July 1996, included alarmist post-plenary changes that did not allow wide scrutiny. Gone from the final report is any meaningful emphasis of the uncertainties about man-made climate change and gone are concerns about unwarranted conclusions being drawn from the studies. In November 1995, the underlying report did not state that human-induced climate change had occurred; now, with no new data to consider, it does (Singer, 1996; *Financial Times*, 1996).

Sentences, such as the following, were deleted from the report: 'None of the studies has shown clear evidence that we can attribute the observed changes to the specific cause of increases in greenhouse gases.' This statement was replaced with: 'If the observed global mean changes over the last 20 to 50 years cannot be fully explained by natural climate variability, some (unknown) fraction of the changes must be due to human influences' (IPCC SAR, 1995, section 8.4.2.1). The draft conclusion to the report was deleted as well.

Some scientists are absolutely outraged at these alterations and a slanging match has ensued in the journals *Science* and *Nature* and the quality press. Dr Frederick Seitz, former head of the US National Academy of Sciences, considers that:

'In my more than 60 years as a member of the American scientific community...I have never witnessed a more disturbing corruption of the peer-review process than the events that led to this IPCC report' (Seitz, 1996).

It is worth noting that the 1995 IPCC report also allowed unpublished papers to be the basis of its conclusions. For example, Chapter 6 of the Second Assessment Report contains 22 references to papers that had not passed peer-review at the time of publication. I asked the head of the scientific working group of the IPCC about peer-review and post-plenary changes when I debated with him in December 1996. His answer was revealing. He acknowledged that they were not peer-reviewed but they were readily available to all IPCC reviewers. But IPCC reviewers would have had to know about these papers – which most did not – and then request them. Any wider comment on the papers was impossible.

The timing of the deletions and alterations suggests that liberties were taken with procedure, perhaps in order to achieve the required consensus. Policy-makers, and the plethora of impact and socio-economic specialist advisors, welcomed the IPCC conclusions and glossed over the irregularities. Instead they concentrated on attacking the industry lobbyists who pointed the changes out, invoking what is known in the UK as the well-worn 'Keeler Principle': 'Well they would say that wouldn't they?', or dismissing critics as practitioners of 'tobacco science'.

The IPCC has become one of the less credible UN agencies because country officials rely on the exact wording of the report they sign their names to; hence reports should be finished when they are final drafts. It should be clear that post-plenary alterations actually undermine the entire IPCC negotiating process. Government officials will be less likely to approve documents in the future if they are under the impression that they will be tampered with later.

It is interesting to note that the breaches of climate treaty protocol were noticed first in the USA, not in Europe. From my personal research I think there is a greater trust in Europe of hierarchies, especially those that are professional. Consequently, science debate is much less open in Europe than in the US. IPCC officials and other senior scientists can pull rank on any doubters, so that hierarchy determines policy. This is what makes continuing analysis of the various subjects and open debate so important.

Coalitions

One of the more disturbing of recent manifestations, which public choice theory would also predict, is the formation of unusual alliances – coalitions between parties whose short-term and narrow interests coincide. The most egregious example in Europe is between some environmental NGOs and insurance companies. The former want business action and support for their initiatives while the insurers want the world's governments to underwrite risky loans in physically sensitive locations. Ironically, one of the things that public choice would also predict is that although actions, such as the removal of subsidies to fossil fuels, are deemed sensible by most policy-makers, economists and environmentalists, they are only slowly removed because of entrenched interests – the bureaucracy overseeing subsidies, and the subsidy recipients such as German miners or multinational energy companies.

Conclusion

For the past decade the debate has centred on climate forecasts and some climate science. Obfuscation and myth-making have flourished. Consensus is now equated with truth. The source of the science has become more important than the content, and peer-review has been used as a political weapon. Those from business have been decried as special pleaders unless they back green claims, and have even spawned their own fifth columnists (environmental managers) whose own jobs depend on the climate business. Nevertheless, the debate continues.

References

Adler, J. (1995): *Environmentalism at the Crossroads,* Washington DC: Capitol Research Center.

Bate, R. (1996): 'The Political Economy of Climate Change Science,' IEA Environment Briefing No. 1, July, London: Institute of Economic Affairs.

Boehmer-Christiansen, S. (1996): 'Political Pressure in the Formation of Scientific Consensus', in Emsley (1996).

Csada, R.D., Jams, P. C. and Espie, R. H. M. (1996): 'The "file drawer problem" of non-significant results: does it apply to biological research?', *Oikos*, Vol. 76 (3).

Emsley, J. (1996): *The Global Warming Debate*, Cambridge: European Science and Environment Forum.

Financial Times (1995): *Climate Change*, Energy Economist Briefings, London: FT Energy Publishing, 1996.

Grubb, M. (1996): 'Purpose and function of IPCC', *Nature*, Vol. 379, p.108.

IPCC (1996): *Summary for Policymakers of the Contribution of Working Group 1 to the Second Assessment Report to the Intergovernmental Panel on Climate Change,* United Nations.

IPCC (1995): *Second Assessment Report*, Approved at the fifth session of IPCC WGI, Madrid, 27-29 November.

Mitchell, W. C. and Simmons, R. T. (1994): *Beyond Politics*, Colorado: Westview Press.

Ridley, M. (1995): 'Climate debate is overheated and full of holes', *Sunday Telegraph*, 10 December.

Seitz, F. (1996): 'A Major Deception on Global Warming', *Wall Street Journal*, 12 June.

Singer, S. F. (1996): 'A Preliminary Critique of IPCC's Second Assessment of Climate Change', in Emsley (1996).

Wilkie, T. (1995): 'Science "using language of the adman",' *The Independent*, London, 1 December .

Winton, N. (1995): 'Global warming theory just hot air, some experts say', *Reuters World Service*, 20 December.

4. Warmer Is Better

Thomas Gale Moore

We can see a lot by looking at history: climate has varied; civilisations have waxed and waned; mankind has prospered in warm periods and suffered in cold.

The world has shifted from periods that were considerably warmer – during the Mesozoic era, when the dinosaurs thrived, the Earth appears to have been about 10°C warmer than it is now – to periods that were substantially colder – during the Ice Ages huge glaciers submerged much of the northern hemisphere (Levenson, 1989, p. 25). During the last interglacial period – about 130,000 years ago or about when modern man was first exploring the globe – the average temperature in Europe was at least 1°C to 3°C warmer than it is at present (Crowley and North, 1991, p. 117). Hippopotamuses, lions, rhinoceroses, and elephants roamed the English countryside. Areas watered today by the monsoons in Africa and East Asia enjoyed even more rainfall. Indeed, during the last 12,000 years – that is, since the end of the last glacial period – the globe has alternated between periods substantially warmer and periods noticeably cooler.

Expected Effects of Global Warming

Although most of the forecasts predict dire repercussions from global warming, an examination of the likely effects suggests little basis for that gloomy view. Climate principally affects agriculture, forestry, and fishing. Manufacturing, most service industries, and nearly all extractive industries are less affected by climate shifts. Banking, insurance, medical services, retailing, education and a wide variety of other services can prosper equally well in warm climates (with air-conditioning) as in cold (with central heating). A few services, such as transportation and tourism, may be more susceptible to weather. A warmer climate will lower transport costs: less snow and ice will torment truckers and automobile drivers; fewer winter storms (bad weather in the

87

summer has less disruptive effects and is over quickly) will disrupt air travel; a lower incidence of storms and less fog will make water transport less risky. A warmer climate could, however, change the nature and location of tourism.

A rise in world-wide temperatures would go virtually unnoticed by inhabitants of the advanced industrial countries. As modern societies have developed a larger industrial base and become more oriented towards services, they have grown less dependent on farming and thus less dependent upon temperature variations.

Only if warmer weather caused more droughts or lowered agricultural output would developing countries suffer. Should the world warm – and there is little evidence or theory to support such a prognostication – most climatologists believe that precipitation would increase. Although some areas might become drier, others would become wetter. Judging from history, Western Europe would retain plentiful rainfall, while North Africa and the Sahara might gain moisture.

A warmer climate would produce the greatest gain in temperatures at northern latitudes and much less change near the Equator. Not only would this foster a longer growing season and open up new territory for farming but it would mitigate harsh weather. The differential between the extreme cold near the poles and the warm moist atmosphere at the Equator drives storms and much of the Earth's climate.

Warmer night-time temperatures, particularly in the spring and autumn, would create longer growing seasons and enhance agricultural productivity. Moreover, the enrichment of the atmosphere with CO_2 would increase the growth rates of most plants. The United States Department of Agriculture, in a cautious report, reviewed the likely influence of global warming on crop production and the world's food prices. The study, which assumed that farmers fail to make adjustments (such as substituting new varieties or alternative crops or increasing or decreasing irrigation) to mitigate the effects of warmer, wetter or drier weather, concludes that there would be 'a *slight increase* in world output and a *decline in commodity prices* under moderate climate change conditions' (Kane *et al.*, 1991, p. i, emphasis added).

Forestry is another sector that is potentially subject to change due to an increase in world temperatures. Agricultural economists have examined the effect of a doubling of CO_2 on forestry production. They concluded that increased carbon dioxide would boost the growth of forests.

Historical Evidence

History provides the best evidence for the effect of climate change on humans, plants and animals. The influence of climate on human activities has declined with the growth in wealth and resources but primitive man and hunter-gatherer tribes were at the mercy of the weather, as are societies that are still almost totally bound to the soil. A series of bad years can be devastating. If, as was usual until very recently, transportation is costly and slow, even a regionalised drought or an excess of rain can lead to disaster, although crops may be plentiful a short distance away. Since the Industrial Revolution, climate has been confined to a minor role in human activity.

Studies of climate history show that sharp changes in temperatures over brief periods of time have occurred frequently without setting into motion any disastrous feedback systems that lead either to a runaway heating that would cook the Earth or a freezing that would eliminate all life. In addition, carbon dioxide levels have varied greatly. Data from ice cores exhibit fluctuating levels of CO_2 that do not correspond to temperature changes (Frenzel, 1993, p. 8). Most past periods, however, display a positive relationship between CO_2 and temperature, with a relationship roughly corresponding to that of the general circulation models (GCMs) (Crowley, 1993, p. 23). The warmer periods, except the Holocene of central North America, brought more moisture to the Northern Hemisphere. At the time of the medieval warm period, temperatures in Europe, except for the basin of the Caspian Sea, were 0.5°C to 1.5°C higher and rainfall more plentiful than today (Frenzel, 1993, p. 11).

This historical evidence is consistent with only some of the forecasts of the computer-generated climate models. Most climate estimates indicate that a doubling of CO_2 would generate greater rainfall in middle latitudes, and history shows that warm climates do produce more wet weather (Crowley, 1993, p. 21).

As has been found in the historical record, land temperatures should increase more than water and, thus, strengthen monsoons. The models also predict that the temperature of the sea's surface in the tropics would be higher with increased CO_2 but evidence from the past evinces no such relationship (Crowley, 1993, p. 25).

Climatologists consider that the last Ice Age ended about 12,000 to 10,000 years ago when the glaciers covering much of North America, Scandinavia and northern Asia began to retreat to approximately their current positions. In North America, the glacial covering lasted longer than in Eurasia because topographic features delayed warming. Throughout history, warming and cooling in different regions of the world have not been exactly correlated because of the influence of oceans, mountains, prevailing winds and numerous other factors.

Human progress – a few improvements in hunting tools and some cave art – was incredibly slow during the Ice Age, a period whose length dwarfs the centuries since. Over the last 12 millennia of interglacial warmth, however, man has advanced rapidly. The growth in technology and living standards required a climate more hospitable than that existing throughout that frozen period.

As the earth warmed with the waning of the Ice Age, the sea level rose by as much as 300 feet; hunters in Europe roamed through modern Norway; agriculture developed in the Middle East. For about 3,000 to 4,000 years, the Earth enjoyed what historians of climate call the Climatic Optimum period, a time when average world temperatures – at least in the Northern Hemisphere – were significantly hotter than today. At its height between 4,000 BC and 2,000 BC, the world was 2°C to 3°C warmer than it has been during the 20th century (Lamb, 1968, p. 6). During the relatively short period since the end of glaciation, the climate has experienced periods of stability separated by 'abrupt transition' (Wendland and Bryson, 1974). H.H. Lamb calculates that at its coldest, during the Mini Ice Age, the temperature in central England for January was about 2·5°C colder than it is today (Lamb, 1968, p. 12). He also concludes that in the central and northern latitudes of Europe during the warmest periods, rainfall may have been 10 per cent to 15 per cent greater than it is now and during the coldest periods of the Mini Ice Ages, 5 to 15 per cent less (Lamb, 1988, p. 30). On the other hand, cooler periods usually suffer from more swampy conditions because there is less evaporation.

If modern humans originated 200,000 years ago, why did they not develop agriculture for the first 190,000 years? Even if *Homo Sapiens* originated only 40,000 years ago, people waited 30,000 years to grow their first crops, an innovation that yielded a more reliable and ample food supply. Is it by coincidence that farming developed first in the Middle East, immediately after the end of the last Ice Age?

Most ecologists take the size of the population of a species as an indicator of its fitness and, by this criterion, the domestication of plants and animals improved greatly the fitness of *Homo Sapiens*. Except for a few disastrous periods, the number of men, women and children has mounted with increasing rapidity; only in the last few decades of the 20th century has the escalation slowed. Certainly there have been good times when man did better and poor times when there was suffering, although in most cases these were regional problems. History shows, however, that warm periods have done considerably better than cold periods in terms of human expansion. The warmest period since the end of the last Ice Age produced the highest rate of population growth and in this era agriculture was spreading. Moreover, the Mini Ice Age, which saw the coldest temperatures in the last 10,000 years, underwent the slowest relative population expansion.

Life expectancy is also a good indicator of human well-being. People lived longer during the warm periods of the Neolithic and Bronze ages and of the High Middle Ages of 13th century England, when the climate was more benign. The shortening of lives from the late 13th to the late 14th centuries with the advent of much cooler weather is particularly notable.

In summary, the evidence overwhelmingly supports the proposition that during warm periods, humans prospered. They multiplied more rapidly; they lived longer; and they apparently were healthier. We now turn to a closer examination of the two major warm epochs.

The First Climatic Optimum

Around 9,000 to 5,000 years ago, the earth was much warmer than it is today, perhaps 2°C hotter, or about the average of the various predictions of global warming at the end of the 21st century (Lamb, 1988, p. 22). Although the climate cooled a bit after 3000 BC, it stayed relatively warmer than the modern world until sometime after 1000 BC, when chilly temperatures became more common. During this Climatic Optimum, Europe enjoyed mild winters and warm summers, with a storm belt far to the north. Not only was the region less subject to severe storms, but the skies were less cloudy and the days sunnier.

Although the weather was less stormy, rainfall was more than adequate to produce widespread forests. Western Europe, including parts of Iceland and the Highlands of Scotland, was mantled by great woods (Giles, 1990, p. 133). Until average temperatures dipped temporarily for about 400 years (*c.* 3500 – *c.* 3000 BC), the timber consisted of warmth-demanding trees such as elms and linden in North America and oak and hazel in Europe. These species have never regained their once-dominant position in Europe and America. Not only did Europe enjoy a benign climate with adequate rainfall, but the Mediterranean littoral, including the Middle East, apparently received considerably more moisture than it does today (Claiborne, 1970, p. 324). The Indian subcontinent and China were also much wetter during this period (Lamb, 1982, p. 120).

Compared to cooler periods in the last few thousand years, the Sahara was much wetter and more fertile during the Climatic Optimum (Lamb, 1988, p. 21). Cave paintings from the epoch depict hippopotamuses, elephants, crocodiles, antelopes, and even canoes (Giles, 1990, pp. 115-16). The water level in Lake Chad about 14° north of the Equator in central Africa was some 30 to 40 metres (90 to 125 feet) higher than it is today, indicating much greater precipitation. Ruins of ancient irrigation channels in Arabia, probably from the warmest millennia, derived their water from streams and springs well above current water supplies, indicating a wetter climate (Lamb, 1977/1985, p. 270).

The Southern Hemisphere seems also to have flourished during the warm millennia after the most recent Ice Age: the southern Temperate Zone enjoyed both warmer weather and more moisture than it does currently (Lamb, 1968, p. 61). Australia was consistently wetter than it is today in both the tropical and temperate regions (Lamb, 1982, p. 131). Since the end of that epoch, the great deserts of Australia have expanded and the climate has become both cooler and drier. Apparently most of the other great desert regions of the world enjoyed more rainfall than they now do during the Climatic Optimum. Lamb contends that the period of maximum temperature was also a period of maximum moisture in subtropical and tropical latitudes and a good period for forests in most temperate regions (Lamb, 1982, p. 131). During this warm era, Hawaii experienced more rainfall than it does in the 20th century (Lamb, 1968, p. 61). Even Antarctica enjoyed warmer weather, about 2.5°C to 3°C higher, and during the summer in some of the mountains the weather was warm enough to produce running streams and lakes that have subsequently frozen (Lamb, 1968, p. 62). Nevertheless, the ice sheets remained stable.

The invention of agriculture coincided with the end of the last Ice Age and the melting of the glaciers: archaeologists have found the earliest evidence for husbandry and farming in Mesopotamia around 9000 BC (Claiborne, 1970, p. 243). The domestication of plants appears to have occurred around the world at about the same time:

'One of the few variables that would seem to be shared is timing: early experiments at plant domestication occurred in Southwest Asia, east Asia, and Central America during the period between 8000 BC and 5500 BC' (Ammerman and Cavalli-Sforze, 1984, p. 16).

The coincidence of the invention of agriculture with a general warming of the climate, an increase in rainfall and a rise in concentrations of atmospheric carbon dioxide – all of which would have made plant growth more vigorous and plentiful – cannot be accidental.

Domestication of plants and animals represented a fundamental shift in man's involvement with nature. Prior to domestication humans simply took what nature offered. People hunted or scavenged the local animals that happened their way. Women gathered fruits and vegetables that grew wild in their territory. With farming and herding, mankind for the first time began to modify his environment. Humans determined what would be grown and which plants would survive in their gardens; which animals would be cultivated and bred and which would be shunned or eliminated. *Homo Sapiens* ceased being simply another species that survived by predation coupled with grazing and became a manager of his environment.

The development of agriculture and the establishment of fixed communities led to a population explosion and the founding of cities. Agricultural societies produce enough surplus to support urban development, the evolution of trade and new occupations – the first step towards specialisation, which lies at the heart of economic advancement (Lamb, 1977/1985, p. 256). Man's taming of animals and plants represents a movement towards establishing property rights. In a hunter-gatherer's world no one owns the wild beasts or the fruit and grains until they are collected. This can work satisfactorily only as long as demands for the resources are quite limited. But, as the literature on the tragedy of the commons shows, once pressures for more grow too large, the resource base can be exhausted. In what is now called North America, many large species, such as horses, were apparently hunted to extinction. Domestication – privatisation of animals and plants – became the answer to over-hunting and over-grazing.

In Europe, the Climatic Optimum produced an expansion of civilisation that brought the construction of cities and a technological revolution when the Bronze Age (3000-1200 BC) replaced the New Stone Age (Lamb, 1982, p. 126). The more benign climate with less severe storms encouraged travel by sea and trade flourished during this warm period. Since the glaciers in the Alps during the late Bronze Age were only about 20 per cent of the size of the glaciers in the 19th century, merchants made their way through the Brenner Pass, the dominant link between northern and southern Europe. Northern Europeans exchanged tin for manufactured bronze from the south, alpine peoples mined gold and traded it for goods crafted around the Mediterranean and Baltic amber found its way to Scotland.

During the warm period prior to 3000 BC, China enjoyed much warmer temperatures. Bamboo, valued for food, building material, writing implements, furniture and musical instruments, grew much farther north – about 3° in latitude – than is now possible (Ko-chen, 1973, pp. 228-29). In Louisiana, archaeologists have discovered a 5,400-year-old monumental earthen structure that suggests a society with ample food and manpower (*San Jose Mercury News*, 19 September 1997, p. 19A). An unknown centralised tribal group must have organised the tremendous effort required to build this edifice.

Prior to the period about 2500 to 1750 BC, north-western India, which is now very dry, enjoyed greater rainfall than it has done during the 20th century (Lamb, 1977/1985, p.251). In the Indus Valley, the Harappas created a thriving civilisation that reached its apogee during the warmest and wettest periods, when their farmers were growing cereals in what is now a desert (Lamb, 1977/1985, p. 389). The area was well watered with many lakes. This civilisation disappeared around 1500 BC at a time when the climate became distinctly cooler and drier (Claiborne, 1970, p. 295).

Cooler, More Varied, and Stormy Times

From the end of the Climatic Optimum of sustained warmth until around 800 AD to 900 AD, the climate of that part of the Earth for which we have data and, in particular, the climate of Europe varied between periods of warmth and cold. Based on the height of the upper tree lines in the mountains of the middle latitudes, the temperature record following the peak warm period around 5000 BC demonstrates a more or less steady decline down to the 20th century (Lamb, 1982, p. 118, Fig. 43). Tree-ring data for New Zealand indicate that after temperatures reached a maximum around 6000 to 8000 BC, the climate cooled in that part of the world (McGlone *et al.*, 1993, p. 311).

After 1000 BC, the climate in Europe and the Mediterranean cooled sharply and by 500 BC had fallen to modern average temperatures (Lamb, 1988, p. 22). The period from 500 BC to 600 AD was one of varied warmth, although cooler on average than the previous 4,500 years. During the centuries of varied weather, classical Greece flourished and then declined and the Roman Empire spread its authority through much of what is now Europe, the Middle East and North Africa. The climate became more clement and somewhat more stable from 100 BC to 400 AD, one of the most economically prosperous periods of the Roman Empire (Lamb, 1988, p. 23). The Italians grew grapes and olives farther north than they had prior to this period. Towards the end of the period, the Roman Empire suffered attacks by barbarians from central Asia, whose eruption out of their homeland may have been brought on by a change in the climate.

From around 550 AD to 800, Europe suffered through a colder, wetter and more stormy period. As the weather became wetter, peat bogs formed in northern areas (Lamb, 1968, p. 63). The population abandoned many lakeside dwellings while mountain passes became choked with ice and snow, making transportation between northern Europe and the south difficult. The Mediterranean littoral and North Africa dried up, although they remained moister than they are now. Inhabitants of the British Isles between the 7th and the 9th centuries were often crippled with arthritis while their predecessors during the warmer Bronze Age period suffered little from such an affliction.

The High Middle Ages and Medieval Warmth

From around 800 AD to 1200 or 1300, the globe warmed considerably and civilisation prospered. This Little Climatic Optimum generally displays, although less distinctly, many of the same characteristics as the first Climatic Optimum (Lamb, 1968, p. 64). Virtually all of northern Europe, the British Isles, Scandinavia, Greenland, and Iceland were considerably warmer than at present. The Mediterranean, the Near East, and North Africa, including the Sahara, received more rainfall than they do today (Lamb, 1968, pp. 64-65). North America enjoyed better weather during most of this period. China during the early part of this epoch experienced higher temperatures and a more clement climate. From Western Europe to China, East Asia, India, and the Americas, mankind flourished as never before.

The timing of the medieval warm spell, which lasted no more than 300 years, was not synchronous around the globe. For much of North America, for Greenland and in Russia, the climate was warmer between 950 and 1200 (Lamb, 1977/1985, p. 435). The warmest period in Europe appears to have been later, roughly between 1150 and 1300, although parts of the 10th century were quite warm. Evidence from New Zealand indicates peak temperatures from 1200 to 1400. Data on the Far East is meagre but mixed. Judging from the number of severe winters reported per century in China, the climate was somewhat warmer than normal in the 9th, 10th, and 11th centuries, cold in the 12th and 13th and very cold in the 14th. Chinese scholar Chu Ko-chen reports that the 8th and 9th centuries were warmer and received more rainfall but that the climate deteriorated significantly in the 12th century (Ko-chen, 1973, p. 235). This record suggests that the Little Climatic Optimum began in Asia in the 8th or 9th centuries and continued into the 11th. The warm climate moved west, reaching Russia and central Asia in the 10th through to the 11th centuries and Europe from the 12th to the 14th. Some climatologists have theorised that the Mini Ice Age also started in the Far East in the 12th century and spread westward, reaching Europe in the 14th (Ko-chen, 1973, pp. 239-40).

Europe

The warm period coincided with an upsurge of population almost everywhere. For centuries during the cold damp 'dark ages', the population of Europe had been relatively stagnant. Although we lack precise census data, the figures from Western Europe after the climate improved show that cities grew in size, new towns were founded and colonists moved into relatively unpopulated areas. As John Keegan, the eminent military historian, put it:

'The mysterious revival of trade between 1100 and 1300, itself perhaps due to an equally mysterious rise in the European population from about 40,000,000 to about 60,000,000, in turn revived the life of towns, which through the growth of a money economy won the funds to protect themselves from dangers beyond the walls' (Keegan, 1993, p. 149).

Written records confirm that the warmer climate brought drier and consequently healthier conditions to much of Europe (Bartlett, 1993, p. 155). With a more equable climate, people spent longer periods outdoors and food supplies were more reliable. Even the homes of the peasants would have become

97

warmer and less damp. The draining or drying up of marshes and wetlands reduced the breeding grounds for mosquitoes that brought malaria. As a result, the infant and childhood mortality rate must have fallen, causing an explosion in population.

The 12th and 13th centuries witnessed a profound revolution that, by the end of the 14th century, had transformed the landscape into an economy filled with merchants, vibrant towns and great fairs. Crop failures became less frequent; new territories were brought under control. With a more clement climate and a more reliable food supply, the population mushroomed. Even with the additional arable land permitted by a warmer climate, the expansion in the number of mouths exceeded farm output: food prices rose while real wages fell. Farmers, however, did well since there was more ground under cultivation and low wages payable to farmhands (Donkin, 1973, p. 90).

The warmth of the Little Climatic Optimum made territory farther north cultivable. In Scandinavia, Iceland, Scotland, and the high country of England and Wales, farming became common in regions that had never before yielded crops reliably and have never done so since. In Iceland, oats and barley were cultivated. In Norway, farmers were planting further north and higher up hillsides than at any time for centuries. Greenland was 2°C to 4°C warmer than at present and settlers could bury their dead in ground that is now permanently frozen. Scotland flourished during this warm period with increased prosperity and construction (Lamb, 1977/1985, p. 437). Greater crop production meant that more people could be fed, and the population of Scandinavia exploded (Claiborne, 1970, pp. 348-64). The rapid growth in numbers in turn propelled and sustained the Viking explorations and led to the foundation of colonies in Iceland and Greenland.

The warm, rainier climate also benefited Europe south of the Alps, especially Greece, Sicily and southern Italy. All of the *Mezzogiorno* in the Middle Ages did well (Cheetham, 1981, p. 37). The Mediterranean flourished in the 12th century. Cordova, Palermo, Constantinople and Cairo all thrived, engendering great tolerance for contending religions (Cheetham, 1981, pp. 35-36). Christian communities survived and prospered in Moslem Cairo and Cordova. The rulers of Byzantium countenanced the Moslems and often preferred them to the barbaric Western Europeans.

In the west, Charlemagne, creator of the Holy Roman Empire, began the cultural renaissance that led to the High Middle Ages, which found summation and closure in Dante's *Divine Comedy*. In *A History of Knowledge*, Charles Van Doren contended that the 'three centuries, from about 1000 to about 1300, became one of the most optimistic, prosperous, and progressive periods in European history' (Van Doren, 1991, p. 111). All across Europe, the population went on an unparalleled building spree, erecting at huge cost cathedrals that we still regard with awe, as well as many other public edifices. Romanesque churches were replaced in the 12th century by Gothic cathedrals. In southern Spain, the Moors laid the cornerstone in 1248 for perhaps the world's most beautiful fortress, the *Alhambra*. It took a prosperous society to launch such major architectural projects.

Economic activity blossomed throughout the continent. Banking, insurance, and finance developed, a money economy became well established, and manufacturing of textiles expanded to levels never seen before. Farmers were clearing forests, draining swamps and expanding food production to new areas (Bartlett, 1993, p. 2). The building spree mentioned above was made possible by low wages, resulting from a population explosion, and by the riches that the new merchant classes were creating. With the clergy still opposing buying and selling for gain, those who became wealthy often constructed churches or willed their estate or much of it to religious institutions as acts of redemption (Pirenne, N.D., p. 50). Such people supplied much of the funds to erect the great Gothic cathedrals.

Starting in the 11th century, European traders developed great fairs that brought together merchants from all over Europe. At their peak in the 13th century, these fairs were located on all the main trade routes and not only served to facilitate the buying and selling of all types of goods but also functioned as major money markets and clearing houses for financial transactions. The 14th century saw the waning of these enterprises, probably because the weather became so unreliable and poor that transport to and from these locations with great stocks of goods became impracticable. Wet, muddy roads rendered arduous the transport of heavy goods. Crop failures made for famines and more vagabonds who preyed on travellers.

During the High Middle Ages, technology grew rapidly. New techniques expanded the use of the water mill, the windmill, and coal for energy and heat. Sailing improved through the invention of the lateen sail, the sternpost rudder and the compass. Governments constructed roads and contractors developed new techniques for use of stone in construction. New iron-casting techniques led to better tools and weapons. The textile industry began employing wool, linen, cotton, and silk and, in the 13th century, developed the spinning wheel. Soap, an essential for hygiene, came into widespread use in the 12th century. Mining, which had declined since the time of the Romans, at least partly because the cold and snow made access to mountain areas difficult, revived after the 10th century.

Farmers and peasants in medieval England launched a thriving wine industry south of Manchester. Good wines demand warm springs free of frosts, substantial summer warmth, sunshine without too much rain, and sunny days in the autumn. Winters cannot be too cold – not below 0°C for any significant period. The northern limit for grapes during the Middle Ages was about 300 miles above the current commercial wine areas in France and Germany. These wines were not simply marginal supplies, but of sufficient quality and quantity that, after the Norman Conquest, the French monarchy tried to prohibit British wine production (Lamb, 1977/1985, p. 277).

Europe's riches and a surplus of labour enabled and emboldened its rulers to take on the conquest of the Holy Land through a series of Crusades starting in 1096 and ending in 1291. The Crusaders, stimulated at least in part by a mushrooming population and an economic surplus large enough to spare men to invade the Muslim empire, captured Jerusalem in 1099 –a feat not equalled until the 19th century. A major attraction of the first crusade was the promise of land in a 'southern climate' (Keegan, 1993, p. 291).

Even southern Europe around the Mediterranean enjoyed a moister climate than it currently does (Langer, 1968, p. 8). In the reign of the Byzantine Emperor Manuel I Comnenus (1143-

1180), art and culture flourished and all the world looked to Constantinople as its leader (Lamb, 1968, p. 269). Under the control of the Fatimid caliphate, Egypt cultivated a 'House of Science', where scholars worked on optics, compiled an encyclopaedia of natural history, with a depiction of the first known windmills, and described the circulation of the blood. In Egypt block printing appeared for the first time in the West (Langer, 1968, pp. 206, 286). The caliphate turned Cairo into a brilliant centre of Moslem culture. In Persia, Omar Khayyam published astronomical tables, a revision of the Muslim calendar, a treatise on algebra and his famous *Rubáiyát* (Carruth, 1993, p. 161).

As European commerce expanded, traders reached the Middle East, bringing back not only exotic goods, but new ideas and information about classical times. The University of Bologna, possibly the oldest university in continuous existence, was founded for the study of the law in 1000 AD. Early in the 12th century, a group of scholars under a licence granted by the chancellor of Notre Dame began to teach logic, thus inaugurating the University of Paris. A community of scholars formed in Oxford at the end of the 12th century and Cambridge University's roots can be traced to 1209, when a group of scholars fled there from Oxford.

Secular writing began to appear throughout northern Europe. In the 12th century the medieval epic of chivalry, the *Chanson de Roland,* was put into writing. Between 1200 and 1220, an anonymous French poet composed the delightful and optimistic masterpiece, *Aucassin et Nicolette*. An anonymous Austrian wrote in Middle High German the *Nibelungenlied* (Carruth, 1993, pp. 134, 170-71).

The Arctic

From the 9th through the 13th centuries, agriculture spread into northern Europe and Russia where earlier it had been too cold to produce food. In the Far East, Chinese and Japanese farmers migrated north into Manchuria, the Amur Valley and northern Japan (McNeill, 1963, p. 559). The Inuit apparently expanded throughout the Arctic area during the medieval warm epoch (Lamb, 1977/1985, p. 248).

At the same time that the Inuit were moving north, Viking explorers were venturing into Greenland, along the eastern coast of North America ('Vinland', probably located in north-eastern Newfoundland or on the coast of Labrador) and even into the Canadian Arctic. Scandinavian sailors found Iceland in 860, Greenland around 930, and reached the shores of North America by 986 (Lamb, 1977/1985, p. 252). By the turn of the millennium, when the waters southwest of Greenland may have been at least 4°C warmer than they are now, Vikings were regularly visiting 'Vinland' for timber (Lamb, 1988, p. 159). At the height of the warm period, Greenlanders were growing corn and some cultivated grain.

The Far East

As noted above, the warming in the Far East seems to have preceded that in Europe by about two centuries. Chinese economist Kang Chao has studied the economic performance of China since 200 BC. In his careful investigation, he discovers that real earnings rose from the Han period (206 BC to 220 AD) to a peak during the northern Sung dynasty (961 to 1127 AD) (Chao, 1986, p. 219). This coincides with other evidence of longer growing seasons and a warmer climate. Chao reports that the number of major floods averaged fewer than four per century in the warm period from the 9th through to the 11th century, while the average number was more than double that figure during the Mini Ice Age of the 14th to 17th centuries (Chao, 1986, p. 203). Not only floods but droughts were less common during the warm period.

The wealth of this period gave rise to a great flowering of art, writing, and science. The Little Climate Optimum witnessed the highest rate of technological advance in Chinese history. During the 300 years of the Sung dynasty, farmers invented 35 major farm implements, which is more than 11 per century, a significantly higher rate of invention than in any other era (Chao, 1986, p. 195). In the middle of the 11th century, the Chinese invented movable type employing clay pieces (Carruth, 1993, p. 151).

During the northern Sung dynasty, Chinese landscape painting with its exquisite detail and colour reached a peak never again matched (Langer, 1968, p. 366). Adam Kesseler, curator of the Los Angeles County Museum of Natural History, dates the earliest Chinese blue-and-white porcelain to the 12th century (Kesseler, 1994, p. A17). The southern Sung dynasty produced pottery and porcelains unequalled in subtlety and sophistication. Literature, history and scholarship flourished as well. Scholars prepared two great encyclopaedias, compiled a history of China, and composed essays and poems. Mathematicians developed the properties of the circle.

Japan also prospered during the Little Climatic Optimum. In the Heian Period (794 to 1192 AD), the arts thrived as emperors and empresses commissioned vast numbers of Buddhist temples. Murasaki Shikibu, perhaps the world's first female novelist, composed Japan's most famous book, *The Tale of Genji*. Other classical writers penned essays: Sei Shonagon, another court lady, wrote *Makura-no-Soshi* (the Pillow Book).

Over the 400 years between 800 and 1200 AD, the peoples of the Indian subcontinent prospered as well. Society was rich enough to produce colossal and impressive temples, beautiful sculpture, and elaborate carvings, many of which survive to this day (McNeill, 1963, p. 559). Seafaring empires existed in Java and Sumatra, reaching their height around 1180. Ninth-century Java erected the vast *stupa* of Borobudur; other temples – the Medut, Pawon, Kelasan and Prambanan – originate in this era. In the early 12th century, the predecessors of the Cambodians, the Khmers, built the magnificent temple of Angkor Wat (Langer, 1968, p. 372). In the 11th century, Burmese civilisation reached a pinnacle: in or around its capital, Pagan, between 931 and 1284, succeeding kings competed in constructing vast numbers of sacred monuments and even a library (Deland, 1987, pp. 9, 29-32).

The Americas

Much of the currently arid areas of North America were apparently wetter during this epoch. Radiocarbon dating of tree rings indicates that warmth extended from New Mexico to northern Canada. In Canada, forests extended about 60 miles north of their current limit (Lamb, 1988, p. 42).

Starting around 800 to 900 AD, the indigenous peoples of North America extended their agriculture northward up the Mississippi, Missouri, and Illinois river basins. They grew corn in northwestern Iowa prior to 1200 in an area that is now marginal for rainfall (Lamb, 1982, p. 177). The Anasazi civilisation of Mesa Verde flourished during the warm period but the cooling of the climate at the end of the medieval warmth around 1280 probably led to its disappearance (Gore, 1992, p. 78). Around 900, the Chimu Indians in South America developed an extensive irrigation system on Peru's coast to feed their capital of between 100,000 to 200,000 souls – a huge number for the era (Carruth, 1993, pp. 142-43).

Thus warmer times brought benefits to most people and most regions but not to all. Nevertheless, for most of the known world the Little Climatic Optimum of the 9th through the 13th centuries brought significant benefits to the local populations; compared with the subsequent cooling it was paradise.

The Mini Ice Age

The Little Ice Age is even less well defined than the medieval warm period. Climatologists are generally agreed that, at least for Europe, North America, New Zealand and Greenland, from 1300 to around 1800 or 1850 temperatures fell, although with many ups and downs. The end of this period of increasingly harsh temperatures could have been as early as 1700, or as late as 1900 for Tasmania. The worst period for most of the world occurred between 1550 and 1700 (Lamb, 1977/1985, p. 463).

The Little Ice Age, especially the century and a half between 1550 and 1700 – the exact timing varied around the globe – produced low temperatures throughout the year and considerable variation in weather from year to year and from decade to decade. It included some years that were exceptionally warm (Lamb, 1977/1985, pp. 465-66). The polar cap expanded, as did the circumpolar vortex, driving storms and the weather to lower latitudes. Although much of Europe experienced greater wetness than it had during the earlier warm epoch, this dampness was more the product of less evaporation due to the cold than an excess of precipitation.

The cooling after the High Middle Ages can be seen in the lowering of tree lines in the mountains of Europe, changes in levels of oxygen isotopes, and advances of the glaciers and of sea ice. As a result of an expanded ice cap, the circumpolar vortex, which funnels weather around the globe, moved south and spawned increasingly cold and stormy weather in middle latitudes. During the coldest period of the 17th century, snow fell above 10,000 feet on mountains of Ethiopia that today never see snow. The subtropical monsoon rains decreased and receded farther south, causing droughts in East Asia and parts of Africa (Fairbridge, 1984, pp. 181-90).

The expansion of the circumpolar vortex produced some of the greatest windstorms ever recorded in Europe: a terrible tempest destroyed the Spanish Armada in 1588; fierce gales wracked Europe in December 1703 and again on Christmas Day 1717 (Lamb, 1988, p. 158). The contrast between the cold northern temperatures that moved south and the warm subtropical Atlantic undoubtedly generated a fierce jet stream.

As early as 1250, floating ice from the East Greenland ice cap was hindering navigation between Iceland and Greenland (Lamb, 1988, p. 159). Over the next century and a half, the prevalence of icebergs became worse and by 1410 sea travel between the two outposts of Scandinavia had ceased. For about 350 years – from the third quarter of the 15th century until 1822 – no ships found their way to Greenland and the local population perished (Lamb, 1988, p. 159).

The deteriorating climate in Europe was heralded by harvest failure in the last quarter of the 13th century. Average yields, which were already low by modern standards, worsened after the middle of the century (Donkin, 1973, p. 91). One of the first severe bouts of cold wet weather afflicted Europe from 1310 to 1319, leading to large-scale crop failures (Lamb, 1977/1985, p. 454). Food supplies deteriorated sharply, generating famine for much of Europe from 1315 to 1318 and again in 1321 (Donkin, 1973, p. 90). Harvest deficits and hunger preceded the Black Death by 40 years. According to Lamb, for much of the continent, 'the poor were reduced to eating dogs, cats and even – children' (Lamb, 1977/1985, p. 266). The history of many villages shows that they were abandoned before the plague

105

began and not afterwards. By 1327, the population in parts of England – especially those later devastated by the plague – had fallen by 67 per cent (Lamb, 1977/1985, p. 7). Between 1693 and 1700 in Scotland, seven out of the eight harvests failed and a larger percentage of the population starved than died in the Black Death of 1348-1350 (Lamb, 1977/1985, p. 454). Those who were poorly nourished were quickly carried off by disease (Lamb, 1977/1985, p. 471).

In two terrible years, 1347 and 1348, famine struck northern Italy (Lamb, 1977/1985, p. 317) and bubonic plague spread across the Alps after 1348, killing in the next two years about one-third of northern Europe's people. Life expectancy fell by 10 years in a little over a century, from 48 years in 1280 to 38 years in the years 1376 to 1400 (Lamb, 1982, p. 189). Crops often failed; peasants abandoned many lands that had been cultivated during the earlier warm epoch. Between 1300 and 1600 the growing season shrank by three to five weeks with a catastrophic impact on farming (Lamb, 1988, p. 32). The capitals of both Scotland and Norway moved south before both areas lost their autonomy.

The cooling after 1300 may also have contributed to the bubonic plague, the greatest disaster ever to befall Europe. Historians have estimated that as many as one-third of all the people in Europe died in the raging epidemic that swept the continent (Lamb, 1977/1985, p. 262). This outburst of the plague, like a similar one in the 6th century, occurred during a time of increasingly cool, stormy, wet periods followed by dry, hot periods. The unpleasant weather is likely to have confined people to their homes where they were more likely to be exposed to the fleas that carried the disease. In addition, the inclement weather may have induced rats to take shelter in human buildings, exposing their inhabitants to the bacillus.

The poorer climate in Europe after the 13th century brought a halt to the economic boom of the High Middle Ages. Innovation slowed sharply (Gimpel, 1983, p. 150). Except for military advances, technological improvements ceased for the next 150 years. Population growth not only ended but, with starvation and the Black Death, fell. Without the drive of additional numbers of people, colonial enterprise ceased and no new lands were reclaimed nor towns founded. The economic slump of 1337 brought on the collapse of the great Italian bank, Scali, leading to one of the first recorded major financial crises (Gimpel, 1983, p. 151). Construction of churches and cathedrals halted.

The hardships of the 14th century induced a search for scapegoats. In 1290, after some years of crop failures, the king of England expelled the Jewish population from the country. The French king followed this example in 1306 and again in 1393 (Pirenne, N.D., p. 134). In 1349, the Christians of Brabant massacred the local Jews and expelled the remainder 21 years later.

The Mini Ice Age at its coldest devastated the fishing industry. From 1570 to 1640, during the most severe period, Icelandic documents record an exceptionally high number of weeks with coastal sea ice. Except for a few years, fishermen from the Faeroe Islands suffered from a lack of cod between 1615 and 1828, since cod needs water warmer than 2°C to flourish. During the worst periods, 1685 to 1704, fishing off southwest Iceland failed altogether (Lamb, 1988, pp. 153-55).

The cold also had devastating effects elsewhere in the world. In China, frosts killed the orange trees in Kiangsi province between 1646 and 1676 (Lamb, 1977/1985, p. 471). Incomes per head fell as food prices rose. Despite the development of a new type of rice that permitted the cultivation of three rather than two crops a year on the same land, the population of China, as well as that of Korea and the Near East, declined for two centuries after 1200, undoubtedly reflecting a deteriorating climate (Carruth, 1993, pp. 166-68).

From around 1550 to 1700 the globe suffered from the coldest temperatures since the last Ice Age. Lamb estimates that in the 1590s and 1690s the average temperature was 1.7°C below the present. Grain prices increased sharply as crops failed. Famines were common. The Renaissance had ended; Europe was in turmoil. The Continent suffered from cold and rain, which produced poor growing conditions, food shortages, famines and finally riots in the years 1527 to 1529, 1590 to 1597, and the 1640s. The shortages between 1690 to 1700 killed millions and were followed by more famines in 1725 and 1816 (Ladurie, 1971, pp. 64-79).

Costs and Benefits of Efforts to Mitigate Warming

Humans, most other animals and, after adjustment, most plants would be better off with a warmer rather than a cooler climate. Not all animals or plants would prosper under these conditions; many are adapted to the current weather and might have difficulty making the transition. Society might wish to help natural systems and various species adapt to warmer temperatures (or cooler, should that occur). Whether the climate will warm is far from certain; that it will change is unquestionable.

Not all regions or all peoples benefit from a shift to a warmer climate: some locales may become too dry or too wet; others may become too warm. Certain areas may be subject to high-pressure systems that block storms and rains; others may experience the reverse. On the whole, though, mankind should benefit from an upward tick in the thermometer. Warmer weather means longer growing seasons, more rainfall overall, and fewer and less violent storms. The optimal way to deal with potential climate change is not to strive to prevent it – a useless activity in any case – but to promote growth and prosperity so that people will have the resources to deal with any shift.

In all probability, if this warming does take place, most people will be better off. On the other hand, if we take the pessimist's view, the costs to the United States, for example, might be as high as 1·5 per cent of its GDP at the end of the next century, although most estimates of the damage from climate change are considerably lower than that figure. The cost of trimming emissions of CO_2 would be much higher. William Cline of the Institute for International Economics – a proponent of major regulatory initiatives to reduce the use of fossil fuels – has calculated that the cost of cutting emissions from current levels by one-third by 2040 as 3·5 per cent of World Gross Product (Cline, 1992, p. 8). Working Group III of the Intergovernmental Panel on Climate Change (IPCC) reviewed various estimates of GDP losses from stabilizing emissions at 1990 levels and concluded that the average projected loss would be 1·5 per cent of the United States' GDP by the year 2050, with the costs increasing more or less linearly with time (IPCC, 1996, p. 307). The IPCC's forecast is for the end of the next century, not the middle. Adjusting for the time difference, the cost to the United States from warming at mid-century would be, at most, only 0.75 per cent, meaning that the costs of holding CO_2 to 1990 levels would be twice the gain from preventing any climate change!

But the benefit to cost calculus is even worse. Returning world-wide emissions to 1990 levels, will not stabilise greenhouse gas concentrations. Since more CO_2 will be added annually for many decades to the atmosphere than the sinks can absorb, the build-up would only slow; consequently, temperatures would continue to go up though by less than would be the case if no steps were taken to reduce CO_2 emissions. Instead, therefore, of saving the full 0.75 per cent of our GDP by keeping emissions at 1990 levels, we would be saving much less, perhaps half as much or 0.375 per cent of our GDP, hardly anything worth worrying about.

It is much easier for a rich country such as the United States to adapt to any long-term shift in weather than it is for poor countries, most of which are considerably more dependent on agriculture than are the rich industrial nations. Such populations lack the resources to aid their flora and fauna in adapting, and many of their farmers earn too little to survive a shift to new conditions. These agriculturally dependent societies could suffer real hardship if the climate were to shift quickly. The best preventive would be a rise in incomes, which would diminish their dependence on agriculture. Higher earnings would provide them with the resources to adjust. Impoverishing Americans to aid a handful of foreign nations will neither help them – we will buy less from them – nor us.

Should warming become apparent at some time in the future and should it create more difficulties than benefits, policy-makers would have to consider preventive measures. Based on history, however, global warming is likely to be positive for most of mankind, while the additional carbon, rain, and warmth should also promote plant growth that can sustain an expanding world population. Global change is inevitable; warmer is better; richer is healthier.

References

Ammerman, A. J. and Cavalli-Sforze, L. L. (1984): *The Neolithic Transition and the Genetics of Populations in Europe*, Princeton: Princeton University Press.

Bartlett, R. (1993): *The Making of Europe: Conquest, Colonization and Cultural Change, 950 – 1350*, Princeton: Princeton University Press.

Carruth, G. (1993): *The Encyclopedia of World Facts and Dates*, New York: Harper Collins.

Chao, K (1986): *Man and the Land in Chinese History: An Economic Analysis*, Stanford: Stanford University Press.

Cheetham, N. (1981): *Mediaeval Greece*, New Haven, CT: Yale University Press.

Claiborne, R. (1970): *Climate, Man, and History*, New York: W.W. Norton.

Cline, W. R. (1992): *The Economics of Global Warming*, Washington, DC: Institute for International Economics.

Crowley, T. J. (1993): 'Use and misuse of the geologic "analogs" concept', in Eddy and Oeschger (1993), pp. 17-27.

— and North, G. (1991): *Paleoclimatology*, New York: Oxford University Press.

Darby, H. C. (ed.) (1973): *A New Historical Geography of England*, Cambridge: Cambridge University Press.

Deland, A. (1987): *Fielding's Far East*, New York: Fielding Travel Books.

Donkin, R. A. (1973): 'Changes in the early Middle Ages', in Darby (1973), Ch.3.

Eddy, J. A. and Oeschger, H. (eds.) (1993): *Global Changes in the Perspective of the Past*, New York: Wiley.

Fairbridge, R.W. (1984): 'The Nile floods as a global climatic/solar proxy', in Mšrner and Karl (1984), pp.181-190.

Frenzel, B. (1993): 'Comparison of interglacial climates regarding space and character', in Eddy and Oeschger (1993), pp. 5-16.

Giles, B. (1990): *The Story of Weather*, London: HMSO.

Gimpel, J. (1983): *The Cathedral Builders*, trans. Teresa Waugh, London: Pimlico.

Gore, A. (1992): *Earth in the Balance,* Boston: Houghton Mifflin.

IPCC (1996): *Climate Change 1995: Economic and Social Dimensions of Climate Change*, Contribution of Working Group III to the Second Assessment Report of the Intergovernmental Panel on Climate Change, James P. Bruce *et al.* (eds.), Cambridge: Cambridge University Press.

Kane, S., Reilly, J. and Tobey, J. (1991): *Climate Change: Economic Implications for World Agriculture*, Agricultural Economic Report No. 647 (October), Washington DC: Resources and Technology Division, Economic Research Service, US Department of Agriculture.

Keegan, J. (1993): *A History of Warfare*, New York: Alfred A. Knopf.

Kesseler, A. T. (1994): 'Exciting Discoveries of Chinese Porcelain', Letter to the Editor, *Wall Street Journal*, 31 May.

Ko-chen, C. (1973): 'A preliminary study on the climatic fluctuations during the last 5,000 years in China', *Scientia Sinica* 16, 2 (May), pp. 226-56.

Ladurie, E. L. R. (1971): *Times of Feast, Times of Famine: A History of Climate since the Year 1000*, Garden City, NY: Doubleday.

Lamb, H. H. (1968): *The Changing Climate,* London: Methuen.

— (1977/1985): *Climatic History and the Future*, Vol. 2 (reprint), Princeton: Princeton University Press.

— (1982): *Climate, History and the Modern World,* New York: Methuen.

— (1980). *Weather, Climate and Human Affairs: A Book of Essays and Other Papers*, London and New York: Routledge.

Langer, W. L. (1968): *An Encyclopedia of World History: Ancient, Medieval, and Modern Chronologically Arranged*, 4th edn., Boston: Houghton Mifflin.

Levenson, T. (1989): *Ice Time: Climate, Science, and Life on Earth*, New York: Harper and Row.

McGlone, M. S., Salinger, J. and Moar, N. T. (1993): 'Paleo-vegetation studies of New Zealand's climate since the last glacial maximum', in Wright *et al*. (1993), pp. 294-317.

McNeill, W. H. (1963): *The Rise of the West: A History of the Human Community*, Chicago: University of Chicago Press.

Mšrner, N. A. and Karl, W. (eds.) (1984): *Climatic Changes on a Yearly to Millennial Basis: Geological, Historical and Instrumental Records*, Dordrecht/Boston: D. Reidel.

Pirenne, H. (N.D., *c*. 1938): *Economic and Social History of Medieval Europe*, New York: Harcourt, Brace.

Van Doren, C. (1991): *A History of Knowledge: Past, Present, and Future*, New York: Ballantine Books.

Wendland, W. M. and Bryson, R. A. (1974): 'Dating climatic episodes of the holocene', *Quaternary Research* 4, pp. 9-24.

Wright, H. E. Jr., Kutzbach, J. E., Webb, T. III, Ruddiman, W. F., Street-Perrott, F. A. and Burtlein, P. J. (eds.) (1993): *Global Climate since the Last Glacial Maximum*, Minneapolis: University of Minnesota Press.